A RARE AND CHALLENGING ENTITY

DR. GEORGE ELTOM

A Rare and Challenging Entity

Copyright © 2025 Dr. George Eltom.

All rights reserved. No part of this publication may be reproduced, stored in a retrieval system, or transmitted in any form or by any means — electronic, mechanical, photocopying, recording, or otherwise — without the prior written permission of the publisher, except in the case of brief quotations used in critical articles or reviews.

This is a work of non-fiction. All memories and accounts are true to the best of the authors' knowledge. Names and identifying details may have been changed for privacy in select instances.

Narrated by
Dr George Eltom

Edited and compiled by
Naami Charlotte Mcaddy

Preface and Afterword by
Naami Charlotte Mcaddy

Photography courtesy of Dr Jennifer Eltom

Hardback ISBN 979 – 8 – 218 – 73959 -1

First edition, Royal Blue Books

To Luke and Sophia, I love you both more than life.

To Jen, I promised I would spend every day making you happy, but it is you who has made me happy every day. I will love you always.

TABLE OF CONTENTS

Preface 7

Introduction 8

PART I 12

    Chapter 1: A George is Born 13

    Chapter 2: Immigration 23

    Chapter 3: Minimum wage, maximum experience 30

    Chapter 4: The Road to Medicine 33

    Chapter 5: The first illness 39

    Chapter 6: Dealing with the unknown 44

    Chapter 7: First visit to Belize 49

    Chapter 8: Mortgage, Medicine and Unexpected Returns 52

    Chapter 9: Return to Belize 55

    Chapter 10: From Scrubs to Gelato... and back again. 63

    Chapter 11: Know Thyself 67

    Chapter 12: The Second Illness 69

    Chapter 13: Between Hope and Surrender 75

    Chapter 14: Telling Luke 79

    Chapter 15: He Who Has a Brother 83

    Chapter 16: My Faith, My Religion 85

    Chapter 17: Messages for a Disconnected World. 90

    Chapter 18: Message to My Colleagues 94

    Chapter 19: The Final Chapter 102

PART II 113

    Chapter 1 114

    Chapter 2 116

    Chapter 3 120

    Chapter 4 122

    Chapter 5 125

    Chapter 6 130

    Chapter 7 133

    Afterword 135

PART III 137

    Reflections..138

PREFACE

George had always planned to write an autobiography; when he received his cancer diagnosis, the idea swiftly shifted from a long-term goal to an urgent priority. As his medical condition deteriorated, it became clear his plan to write and finish this book alone would not be possible. His desire to share his story with the world quickly refocused into a single desire: for his children to know and understand him fully.

Faced with limited time, George chose to record hours of audio and video in his final weeks, a difficult task made harder by fatigue from ongoing treatment and an endless stream of visitors. Yet he pressed on.

The result is this book. Luke and Sophia, it is dedicated to you, every single word. Although incomplete chronologically, it is complete in its message to you. There are so many wonderful aspects to your father that you will discover in the coming years through stories retold by friends and family. This book, however, has a unique purpose: the first part tells your father's story in his own words — where he came from, what shaped him, how he loved, and what he believed. The second part is told by your mother, who continues the story of their life together. Her voice helps complete what your father began, filling in the chapters he could not, and sharing the love they built around you.

Despite his anguish at leaving you both so early, in his final days, the concept of this book brought him peace, knowing that his words will always remain with you. We will never let you forget the great man he was, but if you ever have any doubt, this is here for you to read.

George Eltom

30 December 1981 - 28 July 2024

"I am the resurrection and the life. He who believes in Me, though he may die, he shall live."

John 11:25 NKJV

INTRODUCTION

A research paper described my disease as "a rare and challenging entity." When I read that, I thought those words summarised me well. Rare — not in a grandiose way, but in that I believe we are all rare. No one among the billions on this earth has had the same nature, nurture, challenges, and circumstances that we as an individual has had; that makes us rare in our own way. Challenging — I have always challenged myself to be better, not choosing the easy option or doing things the easy way. I also challenged others to be better, not in a condescending way but rather in the same way I would challenge myself.

Through the book, we will look at events and challenges through my life that helped shape me to the person I am today: immigrating at young age and the culture shock that's involved; setting up a charity and a business, while balancing my life as a family man and a doctor; and finally what appears to be my hardest challenge yet, my current illness.

The reason for writing this book is for my children. Due to the aggressiveness of my disease, it is unclear what the future holds for me, near or distant. Hence, I might not be around as my children grow up to be able for them to know who their father is. I might not have the opportunity to pass on what I learned through my life in person. This book is my way of letting them know who I am and what I learned so they may better know me and hopefully learn from my experiences in a way that may benefit them as they navigate their own lives.

PART I
HIS LIFE IN HIS WORDS

CHAPTER 1
A GEORGE IS BORN

I was born in Sudan in December 1981, the youngest of three boys. Ash and Basil are six and four years older than me, respectively.

From the start, the events preceding my arrival were anything but straightforward. After my brothers were born, my Mum developed a serious back condition. She always wanted a daughter, and despite two miscarriages during subsequent pregnancies (later linked to her lymphoma diagnosis), she persevered. On her third attempt, she conceived again, and although medical advice suggested she terminate due to her back issues, Mum, guided by our Christian faith and consultation with the bishop, decided to continue with the pregnancy. The rest of the pregnancy and delivery went smoothly, and on December 30th, I was born.

By some miracle, my birth improved my Mum's back, and I like to think it meant I was a doctor from day one.

Choosing my name was a predestined affair. Several male members of our family were born on St George's Day (November 17th in the Coptic Church), and traditionally, boys born on that day are named George. However, until I was born, none of the men in our family had been named George. A year or two before my birth, my twin male cousins were born, and despite my Mum's pleas, neither of them were named George. My mother at that time was praying to give birth to a daughter, but she promised that "If God gives me a son, I'll call him George." Although I was born in December, she without hesitation named me George, and St George has been my saint ever since.

My parents have always been role models in my life. They were both very different. My dad was a stoic, proud man. As a young man, he was given a scholarship to university in Germany to study biomedical science. After starting, he realised he didn't have a passion for the subject and switched to interior design. Upon returning home after his degree, there was limited opportunity in that field, so he worked for several years as an accounts administrator.

After the birth of my brothers, he made the decision to open his own company in furniture making. After a slow start, he managed to grow it to a successful business with the support of my mum. Dad was ambitious, motivated, and entrepreneurial. While people in modern times tend to lean towards self-interest and backstabbing, he taught us how to achieve it with hard work, whilst respecting yourself and others. He taught me a lot about never giving up and that it was possible to achieve anything you put your mind to.

My dad was not the best at expressing emotions and at times quick to anger, and some find him scary on first impression. I guess even role models are not perfect. However, he was a very loyal and trustworthy friend to others and made himself approachable to them. Until now, the door is always open to anyone that wants to visit or call. This can be at all times of day, and sometimes in Sudan, we would have visitors arriving at 11 p.m. or even past midnight. This sometimes was a great annoyance to my mum, who then had to host them.

I have many wonderful memories of growing up with my dad. My favorites include nights spent playing backgammon until late. There was always a shout of "one more game," which never went down well with mum, as she was keen to get me to bed on school nights. However, this was my *me* time with Dad, and I wanted it to last as long as possible. I might be the sharing type but not when it comes to family — they are mine! Both of my sisters-in-laws are still trying to come to terms with that!

Another memory, which happened less frequently, was our fishing trips on the banks of the Nile. We didn't really catch anything except catfish, which some might know is not the most glamorous of fish. Most of the time, it was catch and release (before that was even a thing, which it isn't still in Sudan!), except for some of the slightly bigger ones, which I proudly bought home. We'd keep them in the fish tank where they terrified many, given that they were not the prettiest species!

I also enjoyed visiting dad's workshop and watching him work with his hands. Although we didn't go to the factory much, there was something about being around machinery and seeing things made that fascinated me. These moments with my dad were precious, and I believe they had a lasting impact on me.

My mum, on the other hand, had different qualities. She is full of love and kindness, and she will go to hell and back for anyone. An absolute angel that is loved by so many people. She would never put herself first, which for us at times was very frustrating, since we thought she needed to. She worked as a bank teller until I was five, and then she gave it up to became a stay at home mom. It's difficult to think of specific memories from childhood with Mum; she was a consistent presence that always filled me with comfort and love.

The combination of my parents gave me exposure to a wide range of qualities that helped me become the man I am today. I see elements of them in everything I do.

I always considered myself lucky when it came to my family, not just because of my parents, but because of my brothers too. Despite our age difference, we grew up close to each other and were friends, not just brothers. Sometimes, to their annoyance, I felt more comfortable around them and their friends rather than those of my own ages. This was problematic at times, especially when I was a poor student and they had to cover my tab whenever we went out to dinner.

Ash and Basil were very different characters. We all grew up in the church, and we all attended Sunday school, so we had a strong Christian foundation that played a large part in our lives and gave us a degree of common ground. Ash is more "old school," which he got from Dad, and sometimes that scares him. He is risk aversive and his actions are very calculated. (Me, on the other hand, am as far from that as possible!) Basil is somewhere in the middle when it comes to risk. He is also the most like Mum, and he is always Mum's defender whenever there was a difference of opinion with Dad or one of us. This led to us proclaiming Basil as Mum's favourite. I was labelled as Dad's favourite, something he often proudly proclaimed, much to my delight. Admittedly, that list of favourites also included his car and our African grey parrot, Koko, but I always hoped I topped that list! As for Ash, he held the title of being my Granddad's favourite because he was one of the first grandchildren. So, I guess that made it fair for all three of us.

Koko was exceptionally talented at mimicking Dad's voice and enjoyed calling Ash's name. Koko would often shout Ash's name, which then made Ash think Dad was calling. Other times, Ash would ignore Dad calling, since Ash thought it was the bird. Needless to say, Ash learned how to distinguish between the two the hard way!

Growing up with Ash and Basil was fun. We shared a triple bedroom, which made for much entertainment. The three beds were parallel to each other, with the area between the beds labelled the "trenches." We frequently had friends sleep over, which was good when we needed a fourth team member, especially when playing "flip-flop war." Each team of two would take cover in a trench, armed with a stack of flip-flops, and mayhem would follow!

The other advantage of having older brothers was that they were my tickets out of the house, especially on Fridays as we were off school. Bas and me would make an early start around 6 or 7 a.m. to meet up with my cousins and cycle down to the Syrian Social Club. The social club was a hub for everything; it had a large outdoor swimming pool, football field, and basketball court. They catered food and hosted many functions, including weddings and holiday parties. On those Fridays, we would get to the club before it officially opened, make our way to the pool, and spend the whole day there racing, playing games and using the dive board. We would then come out for lunch at midday, and after we digested and rested, go to the football field. There we do exercises and drills followed by five-a-side football games. After food and rest, at 6 p.m., we would then head to the basketball court and play for a few hours, sometimes even squeezing in some volleyball. This was followed by a very painful cycle back home, given that every muscle in our body now ached. However, this meant we were in very good physical shape, a lifestyle that was difficult to replicate when we moved to the UK.

My paternal grandfather was a patriarchal figure in the family. He was a high ranking administrative in the Ministry of Education, an advisor to the then president, so our family name was fairly recognised. He was also an acclaimed poet and songwriter, greatly loved and respected by many. While historically people are not fond of their in-laws, I have never seen my mum so utterly distraught as when he passed away, which shows how he meant to her and to the whole family. Unfortunately, I have very hazy memory of him, given my young age and the fact that he also traveled a lot. Plus, during his last few years, he lived in Abu Dhabi, which limited the time spent with him. He was a typical grandfather, who spoiled us rotten with toys and sweets galore after trips. He had 5 sons, one of which picked up the poetry bug. I myself at times have felt drawn to poetry too, having written primitive poetry at young age and few church plays. This book, however, is my biggest writing project.

If you ask my mum, she will say I was the easiest of her children to raise. Unlike my two elder brothers, I didn't have many tantrums or mischievous phases. I wasn't particularly docile, neither, but somewhere in the middle — not too difficult, not too quiet. I was a fairly active child, a little prone to clumsiness, which led to more than a few serious accidents, especially given the outdoor lifestyle and freedom children in Sudan then had. Homes typically opened into an open courtyard space, where we spent most of our free time playing. I remember running into a big metal door latch, which resulted in a serious head injury. The memory of it still sticks with me: blood everywhere, my dad and grandfather rushing me inside to help. They used powdered coffee as a remedy to stop the bleeding, and I still recall the odd sensation of coffee mixed with blood in my mouth. Despite the injury, I was more focused on the drama of the situation than the pain.

I received several head injuries at that time, though not all of which were my fault, as my cousins were a little mischievous. Bas, who was always my protector, was involved in one of the accidents. I remember an occasion when he had me on his shoulders at school, running around. Of course, he tripped, but as we fell, being the amazing human and brother he is, he covered my face with his hands, protecting me and sacrificing himself.

At school, I was never a troublemaker. I did well academically, perhaps better than as an adult! I wasn't a straight-A student, but I did well and didn't cause my parents too much concern. I wasn't the most popular kid, but I was fine with that, happy to just be myself. I remember I loved organising, even from the age of nine or ten, and I would arrange activities and games. I loved dancing, disco, and socialising, all the way through to my adult life.

I wasn't much of a fighter growing up. However, there was one incident that stands out. When I was about 10, a friend of mine invited me to the market with him. His mother had asked me to deliver an item to the shopkeeper, so I went with him, expecting a simple errand. What I didn't know was that my friend had stolen a piece of gold from his mother and was trying to sell it. I didn't realise it until later, and once I found out, I was furious. I felt betrayed, and we had a physical fight because I was so angry at him for dragging me into something I didn't want to be part of, without my knowledge. That marked the end of our friendship. It was a real learning experience for me, and while it wasn't a mischievous act on my part, it was something I deeply regretted being involved. There were a few other times when I got into fights, particularly when I started school in the UK. I never started fights, but I defended myself when necessary.

I was entrepreneurial even back then. As I mentioned, my paternal grandfather used to bring back us things from all over the world. I remember thinking once that I had to save money for an upcoming trip to London, so I began selling some of the things to raise money. I probably went a bit too far, though. I remember selling a nice set of pens that Bas had and then denied knowledge later. I was no angel, but that was probably one of the worst things I did as a child.

There are also some funny stories from my childhood, particularly involving food. I remember being forced to eat a traditional Arabic dish called *Kishk*, which I absolutely hated. It was a soupy, gooey dish, and as a child, this texture made it impossible for me to enjoy. I remember being at my uncle's house, the dish being served, and me saying, "I don't eat this." It was probably the worst thing I could say to him because he hated wasting food; you absolutely had to eat what was placed before you. He made me finish the whole serving. I don't know how I did it, but I haven't eaten it since, and to this day, I cannot even look at it without remembering that experience.

Another funny food story revolves around my "allergy" to mushrooms and salmon. I am not allergic to those, though. It all started when I was about 10. We used to visit my dad's cousins on big occasions, where there would always be whole salmon as part of the celebrations as well as a mushroom dish. I had learnt from my earlier experiences that refusing to eat would be met with protests or ignored. On the second visit, I said I mentioned that salmon and mushroom did not agree with me and that I thought I might be allergic. On the third occasion that we visited, I was offered the same again, and this time it was Basil who said, "No, he can't eat them he has an allergy." From there it stuck, and it has carried on all these years. Looking back, I think the reason it took off is because of how casually Basil said it. I remember that it almost took me by surprise, like, "Wait. *Am* I allergic?" And then I thought, "Oh yeah, I guess I am." Unbelievably, as yet another testament to how much of a protector he is to me, he doesn't eat either of them because I don't eat them.

I know I paint a picture of a perfect family that's almost too good to be true. At times, it was perfect, but like every family, we had our ups and downs. Being close-knit came with its own challenges; for example, we were deeply involved in one another's lives, which sometimes meant offering opinions that hadn't been asked for, even though these always came from a place of care.

My family will remain one of the greatest sources of support in my life. I always felt puzzled when someone tells me they are estranged from their siblings or parents because the question in my mind would be "How did you survive life without that support?!" However, we all find strength in different places ,and what worked for me might not be the same for others. This brings me back to my introduction — that we are all rare because of the variability in our composition as individuals. It is these experiences of fun and family that have shaped who I am today.

CHAPTER 2
IMMIGRATION

My family's move to England came during political unrest in Sudan. At the time, Sudan was governed by a military regime with strong Islamic beliefs. This was a different regime than the one my grandfather worked for, and Christians were under the microscope. As my father's business grew, it attracted unwanted attention from the local police and government. We had just built a furniture showroom; the design was done by my dad and was modern with a slanted roof. One of the local police chiefs saw it and said that it looked like a church. We explained that it is not a church, but he remained adamant that it looked like a church. He demanded that we flatten the roof. My father refused. Shortly after, Dad didn't come home after work. After a while, we all got worried. After a series of phone calls to contacts, we found out he was taken by the police at a checkpoint for no reason. They kept him for 3 days and then let him go. No reason was given. Dad knew this was all related to the police chief and the roof. To avoid any further hassle, he reluctantly flattened the roof, which broke his heart as he was proud of his initial design.

At this point, he started questioning if staying in Sudan is the right thing for the family and our safety. Shortly after was the introduction of compulsory military service. While military service is usually just more of a training camp, it was made more difficult for the Christians, as they were often put on the frontlines of war. So the decision was made that we would leave Sudan. Our family had a meeting to decide between England and Canada, and we voted for the England. My brothers were sent to London ahead of us, since they were coming of age for military service. I was 12 at this point, so I stayed with my parents.

This is when things got a bit difficult for me emotionally and physically. Emotionally, I no longer had my two brothers to play with, and I was too young to go to the social club on my own. I still had friends and family around, but it wasn't the same without them. Physically, I put on weight because I was at home more often, which meant more food and snacks. The weight gain did not help my emotional state either.

I was eventually reunited with me brothers, but my excitement was dampened as I didn't see much of them as before. Bas was busy studying for Advanced levels, with travel back and forth from college. Ash had started university, and all his hours were also taken up commuting and studying.

I do not know how they managed, but for me, the move to a new education system was quite an adjustment. I had attended a private school in Sudan, an Italian-run institution, predominantly staffed by priests and nuns, although there were also some local Sudanese teachers. The contrast between this and school was striking. Every morning in Sudan, we'd gather for assembly outside, lining up and singing the national anthem. The whole process had military-like precision to it. Then we'd head off to our classes, 30 to 60 students per class. When the teacher entered, we would stand and greet them with a "good morning." Physical punishment was common; the cane or the side of the ruler on the hand was the standard form of discipline, and you didn't need to do much to earn it.

Meanwhile, my new school in England could have easily passed as a young offenders' institution. To set the scene, my future GCSE (General Certificate of Secondary Education) results, as an immigrant, was amongst the highest in the school that year. My first lesson was geography. I walked into the class, which had about 15 or 16 students. Some had their feet up on the desk and were just casually chatting. When the teacher entered, I stood up, as was customary back home, but no one else did. I was completely baffled. No one even acknowledged the teacher's arrival. I stood there, wondering what I was supposed to do. In the end, I did what felt natural to me: I sat down at my desk, and when they said, "Read this, do that," I simply followed the instructions. Before long, I found myself being the teacher's pet in every class.

Maths was one of my favourite subjects. When I was leaving Sudan, we had already begun advanced algebra. After my first maths lesson in my new school, I was promptly excused from all further classes and would spend the lesson in the IT room. Every now and again, there would be a new maths teacher. I remember one teacher who insisted I had to come to class: "He is on the roster. He should be in class." In that lesson, she wrote an equation on the board and asked for volunteers to solve it. No one put their hand up, so I went up and very quickly solved the equation. She promptly responded, "That's fine. You don't need to come to class anymore." It was funny at the time, but looking back, I do have a little bit of regret about how complacent I became. I could have gotten better grades if I pushed myself.

In art and music, however, I was useless. When we had to choose between art and music at GCSE, I went to my music teacher and asked him which subject I should choose. I think his response was, "People choose to look at art. But they don't choose to listen to music if you play it close to them." That was probably the kindest way to say, given my musical skills, I should definitely choose art. As it turns out, that was the better choice, I think — even though I always wanted to learn a new instrument. I also love to sing, but I cannot sing. My art was passable, and I was very proud of my final art project. There was a sphere divided into two sections: one half was a globe, which had Newton sitting with a tree and apple, and the other half was an atom with Einstein, a very geeky artistic representation the two pillars of science.

Starting out, there were a few playground fights. I never faced real physical harm; the comments were the most damaging. It was not easy to make friends at first, and the isolation during those initial months really got to me. I felt alone, and that was tough. However, my church played a crucial role in helping me. I began making friends there, though I didn't realize just how much that support would mean to me until later in life.

Things did eventually improve. We were able to bring my uncle, aunt, and cousins, Nisreen and Sami, to England — not just to London, but to the house next door. The gardens were connected, so it felt like one house. Suddenly, I went from having no one to having essentially an older sister and younger brother, which I always wanted, living next door. They were a massive amount of support both in those early days and throughout my life. Nisreen was especially helpful because she joined my school, and I suddenly had a friend in school, on the bus, and after school. She was also less of a teacher's pet, and more "cool," so she helped me make friends. I never told her, but the difference that made to me was huge.

For Sixth Form, I went to St. Charles, which was in Ladbroke Grove. I was joined there by Michael Takla and Tony Awad, and we became fast friends — the three amigos. It was a completely different experience there. The students were more focused, and I made real friends. At the time, there was no Advanced Subsidiary levels, so it was maths, chemistry, and biology for me. Maths was my strongest subject, followed by chemistry and then biology. I was clumsy, which showed in chemistry; if there was the sound of a beaker breaking, the teacher would shout "George!" and look at me. So I knew early on that being a surgeon was not in the cards for me.

Maths would always have a special place for me, and the teacher who taught Basil maths taught me as well. She felt that both of us had a gift for maths, so to speak. I was really looking forward to sharing my love of maths with Luke.

When I think about how my family and I left our home all

those years ago, it reminds me of current global issues concerning immigration. People don't choose to leave their homes and everything they know for nothing. Something has driven them to do so. They're so scared for their lives, and they are willing to leave everything behind in search of safety. To treat them as second class, after all they have endured, is inhumane. Many of these individuals are highly intelligent and have so much to offer. I like to think that I, too, had something valuable to contribute to my field of study. I can't help but wonder: If this current view on immigration was so prevalent back when we left Sudan, would we even have been given the opportunity that we were? Would we have been welcomed or rejected? I believe we need to take a long, hard look at how we view asylum seekers. I understand there's a system in place, and I know that some people abuse it. But when you look at the majority of people seeking refuge today, it's clear that they are fleeing from situations far beyond their control.

Everywhere you look, there's some form of war or conflict. Take Sudan, for example. How can we ignore the fact that children are being harmed in such turmoil? Every country has its limitations and must prioritize its own citizens, but that doesn't mean we can't show compassion. Sharing a little, helping where we can, it goes a long way. Offering refuge to someone in need, someone who has already suffered so much, is a powerful act of love. It speaks to our humanity.

When my family received our indefinite leave to remain in the United Kingdom, we were overjoyed because it meant the UK was finally our home. It took some time to achieve, which made it even more meaningful. By the time we became UK citizens, we had already lived in the UK for ten years and felt like we belonged, with or without the passport.

When I finally received my British passport, the main feeling was freedom — specifically, freedom to travel. However, I still felt there were restrictions, such as immigration officers routinely inviting me to a "special" queue once Sudan was noted as my place of birth. Nevertheless, I definitely had more options with a whole world now accessible for exploration.

CHAPTER 3
MINIMUM WAGE, MAXIMUM EXPERIENCE

I started working at an early age. I liked to have my own money and with Mum as a housewife and Dad as a self-employed contractor and carpenter, I didn't feel that as a teenager, a young man, that I should be asking for pocket money. I started with paper rounds; later, I found a longer-term position in Cargo Home Stores, which was a furniture store, right next to our flat. I did well there and was eventually offered an assistant manager role, but it was a full-time position, and at that time, leaving full-time education was not an option. I was paid by commission, so my people skills worked well, and I really enjoyed the role.

Later, when we moved to Barnes, I managed to get a job at a pharmacy was run by a lovely Iraqi couple, who were kind and warm-hearted. It was a good place to work, and I ended up staying for quite a while, doing pretty much everything they needed me to do. From time to time, a locum pharmacist would come in, and I have to admit, it always irritated me. As a dispenser, I was responsible for all the prep work. I was earning minimum wage whilst the locum, who made significantly more, would simply sit at a desk and double-check the things I'd carefully prepared. It seemed unfair, but that's how things went. Despite that, I really liked the job. I had plans to become a doctor, and back then, it felt like the closest I could get to being involved in medicine.

After that, I found a similar role on Edgware Road in London. The details of how I landed it are a bit hazy; it was quite a distance from home. Edgware road itself is its own little bubble. It was interesting how businesses there had adapted to the clientele. It had the only Woolworths in the whole country that was opened to midnight, to fit in with the Arab culture. In the shops and banks, all the signs were in Arabic. Being there was comforting, and it became the closest thing to home for me.

One of the most entertaining things I used to do was eat at the local McDonald's. The manager was Italian, who appeared to only recruit fellow Italians, despite his large Middle Eastern client base. Watching these two extremely expressive cultures and languages interact and try and communicate made for an extremely entertaining lunch hour!

The highlight, though, was the many food options in the area. The amazing Shawarma restaurants received most of my salary, and the sandwich shop near my first pharmacy job also received a decent portion of my salary! They made an amazing bacon, sausage, and cheese melt baguette—parbaked bread, fresh and hot, buttered, with the filling melted to perfection. Nothing I've found since has come close!

CHAPTER 4
THE ROAD TO MEDICINE

From a young age, if you asked me what I wanted to be, the answer was always the same: a doctor. It never changed. I never considered anything else, except for being an astronomer, which I thought about for a day.

My mum's cancer diagnosis was one of the biggest influencers of my decision. She had lymphoma before I was born, and she had to travel to the UK for treatment. When she was away, we stayed with my Uncle Rafat, who was a doctor. He also played a huge role in shaping my life. There were many things about him that inspired me, but there's one moment that truly defined my path. I must have been around six or seven years old. We had just finished dinner, around 8 p.m., when the phone rang. It was a woman from quite a distance away, probably an hour or more. Her son had malaria and was very sick. There was a massive sandstorm outside, and in normal circumstances, no one would risk traveling in such weather. But my uncle didn't hesitate. He jumped into his car, drove out through the storm, helped the boy, and came back. To me, that was a superhero move. From that moment, I knew that being a doctor was the only thing I wanted to do. It wasn't about wanting to be a hero, but about seeing the real impact he could have on someone's life. What other job could create that kind of difference? Also, the fact that he did it without a second thought, no fear for his own safety, just focused on helping someone in need, was mind-blowing. He had a family — a wife and children. It showed me that what he did mattered far more than anything else.

When I pursued medicine, I was determined to spend part of my elective with him. Medical electives were our opportunity to gain experience in a specific area of medicine or in a particular setting. By then, he was practicing in Canada, and I learned a lot from him. It was strange, though. Outside of work, he was very impatient and quick to anger. But with his patients, he was completely different. He took time to connect with them, asking about their families, remembering personal details, even learning a bit of their language to greet them. His dedication to understanding his patients, all from different backgrounds, was remarkable. Sometimes, I wonder, without that evening, without seeing him in action, would I have become a doctor? I'm not sure. But he was definitely a huge inspiration.

The path to achieving my dream was far from easy. I had a biology teacher who told me, "You'll never get into medicine." But my dad, on the other hand, encouraged me by saying, "If you put your mind to something and give it your all, you'll get there." I took his advice to heart. When I first I applied for medicine, I essentially got four rejections, with Leicester saying I could contact them once I had my A-level results. They wanted two As and a B. But on results day, I got an A and two Bs, and therefore, they couldn't offer me a place. Despite facing four rejections from medical schools, and hearing that same biology teacher's discouraging words, I couldn't help but question whether I was on the right path. It would have been easier to give up, to listen to those doubts. But instead, those moments only fueled my passion even more.

My advice to anyone pursuing a dream is this: Don't doubt yourself. Don't doubt what's in your heart. If you truly want something, invest in it fully. Put every ounce of effort into it. Because if you do, you'll make it. We are stronger than we often think. So, no matter the obstacles, always follow your heart. Yes, it's been full of ups and downs, but I honestly can't imagine doing anything else. Had I chosen a different path, I don't think I'd have found the same joy. What this journey has given me is not just success; it made me the person I am today.

When I received my A-level results, I was obviously not in the best of moods. Wanting to cheer me up, Basil took me to the cinema, knowing how much I love movies. The movie showing was *Patch Adams*, starring Robin Williams, a true story about a doctor who uses humor and compassion to treat patients in unconventional and deeply human ways. Needless to say, it was not the best choice. I cried throughout the entire film. But, strangely enough, it turned out to be a profound experience. The way Robin Williams' character practiced medicine deeply resonated with me; it was aligned with my own developing philosophy of medicine. I'm sure Basil felt awful that instead of lifting my spirits, *Patch Adams* made me cry, but the movie was also instrumental in shaping my vision and influencing the doctor I am today.

After the realisation that I had no university place, I decided I would take a gap year and reapply the following year. I decided I would spend the year as an event organiser. I enjoyed organising, and at the time, I used to organise every family event. That was my thing. So, my plan was to start that as a business. I already had my pharmacy job, and I thought I could do this alongside. However, my parents were against this idea, believing I wouldn't go back to studying if I took a break, and they would not let the matter drop. During this time of uncertainty, I received a letter about interviewing for biomedical sciences program at St George's Hospital Medical School in Tooting, London. I thought I'd attend, just to keep them my parents happy, but my plan was do everything to I could to make sure I didn't get a place.

During the interview, I was blunt. When they asked why I wanted to do the course, I said, "I don't. I just want to go into medicine." This was followed with "Is there an area in biomedical sciences you're interested in?" I said, "No, not really." After a few more questions, they stepped out and came back in offering me a place. I was shocked. Now I had an offer, and I wasn't sure how to tell my parents that I didn't want it. After a lot of convincing, I reluctantly accepted. That was the beginning of my journey at St George's. Looking back, St George's always stood out to me out of all the places I applied to. I ultimately accepted the biomedical science program, but had it been anywhere else, I probably would have turned it down. It wasn't just the name; it was the feeling that George's was the right fit from the start. I'm fortunate to have found my life's passion.

For my children, Luke and Sophia I want to leave them this advice: If you're unsure about what to dedicate your life to, I believe it's important to go back to the basics. Reflect on what truly makes you tick, what brings you happiness, even if that sounds naïve. Yes, sometimes we have to take jobs we don't love to pay the bills and support our families. But if we can find something that truly resonates with us, it has the potential to bring out the best in us. Identifying your skill set is crucial. It's not about having a specific talent, such as being able to draw and then feeling forced into a career like architecture. Your skill set can be simpler than that.

For example, I would say that my skill set lies in logical thinking — piecing things together. It's not about memorizing diseases and their treatments. It's about understanding the process, the logic behind how things work. I loved maths and science in school. In medicine, I found a way to blend the two. I use the logic I learned from maths—not equations, but the way maths encourages problem-solving. In maths, if you get stuck, you go back to the basics, trying again and again until you solve it. Medicine is no different. When you're stuck, you start with the basics: What symptoms are present? What did the initial tests show? You slowly build a picture and try to piece it all together. If something doesn't add up, you ask yourself, "What else could it be?" This is the same process as solving a maths problem, just with different variables.

There are different ways to think, and logical thinking is just one of them. The key is to identify your own way of thinking. Once you know that, you can look for careers that align with your natural skills. Then you can explore and brainstorm, finding a path that fits. Without knowing your core skill set, you can see what careers align with it, and that will more likely bring you better fulfilment than anything else.

This has been my approach to problem-solving in life in general: to apply logic. I teach medicine the same way. I tell junior doctors, "When you look at the big picture, it's easy to panic. Break it down to the basics, and work your way through it." Instead of focusing on every result in isolation, I remind them to step back, ask basic questions, and slowly build the puzzle.

CHAPTER 5

THE FIRST ILLNESS

Shortly after my 21st birthday, I started experiencing headaches. I was in the first semester of my third year of my biomedical science degree. Initially, I didn't think much of them, but soon they became constant and increasingly severe. I went to my general practitioner (GP), who diagnosed them as tension headaches, advising rest and time off. I followed the recommendation for about a week, but the headaches only worsened. One day, they became so unbearable that Bas took me back to the GP. I was struggling to walk, and keeping my eyes open was a challenge. It was rough. The GP still insisted they were tension headaches, but Bas wasn't convinced. So, Bas decided to take matters into his own hands and drove me to Kingston A&E. On the way there, I vomited—quite violently, and some even went into the air vent. No matter how much Bas tried to clean it, for weeks afterward, every time he turned on the air conditioning, the car smelled of vomit.

By the time he got me to A & E, he was practically carrying me. The receptionist took one look at me and placed me straight onto a stretcher. I had a CT, which didn't show anything, so the medical team decided to do a lumbar puncture. For me, with needles, I always have to see the needle. If you tell me to look away from the needle, I get very anxious and sweaty. I have to look. But with a lumbar puncture, there was no way of looking at the needle. So, I ended up lying on my side to have this lumbar puncture with Bas in front of me, to reassure me, but I could tell he wasn't handling it well. His paleness didn't help my nerves.

I stayed in the hospital for more tests. There was one day when I was barely conscious — my Glasgow Coma Scale (GCS) score of 13 with me drifting in and out of awareness, seeing my family gathered around me. The decision was made to transfer me to Charing Cross Hospital for a neurology opinion. Once there, I encountered a registrar who I'd met before. He was a nice guy, easygoing, and we had a good rapport. However, one day, he came in, drew all the curtains around me, and sat down in front of me. The action filled me with dread. The main
diagnosis at the time was benign intracranial hypertension (BIH). However, given I was a 21-year- old young man, it would be very atypical. I waited for him to tell me the actual cause was more sinister, but then he said, "The tests are inconclusive. We just need to do more to understand what is going on." I was so relieved. I told him I had feared the worst, but he reassured me that there was no definitive answer yet.

We went through several more tests, including MRIs. The

doctors weren't sure whether it might have been a thrombus, but they couldn't confirm it. In the end, they decided to treat it as BIH, the condition I didn't quite fit the typical profile for. I was started on Acetazolamide, a medication to reduce the pressure in my brain. However, because of the severity of the condition, I was also required to undergo monthly therapeutic lumbar punctures until my condition stabilized.

Six months later, while playing football, I suffered a leg injury and developed pain in my calf which didn't settle. I went to A&E. Initially I was diagnosed with a gastrocnemius tear. An ultrasound was arranged to evaluate, but instead of a tear, it demonstrated a deep vein thrombosis (DVT), which was a surprise. When I went back to my follow-up to my neurologist, I said, "Look, if this is a clot, then I must have had a brain clot. It must be a related thing. He agreed. There was no provocation for DVT in my case, the pain had started on the spot. And so, he recommended a haematology opinion.

I was referred to the haematologist at St George's. Tests showed that my DVT kept progressing and that I continued to clot despite being on anticoagulation. They couldn't quite explain it. One day, I experienced chest pain and went into hospital. I ended up with having a CTPA, which showed I had a pulmonary embolism, so a decision was made to place an IVC filter.

Soon after, on my 22nd birthday, we were at home in Hampton with friends and family, about to go to dinner. Then I felt a tickle at the back of my throat. I went to the bathroom to try and clear my throat. I coughed and painted the bathroom red. I yelled for Bas. He came and nearly collapsed when he saw the blood. Then he went and called a friend of ours, who came quickly to assess me. We found ourselves quickly back in A & E where I spent my birthday with my friends in the waiting room singing "happy birthday." Eventually, tests showed that I bronchial artery aneurysm that had bled, which required embolisation to stop the bleeding. It was to be one of many eventful birthdays.

Initially, the hospital admissions were short, a few days to weeks. But the admissions got longer, until one point I was in hospital for 4 months. All of this was happening in the final year of my biomedical science degree. I still had to revise, prepare for the medicine interviews, do my final project, and write up my dissertation. These were crucial for my admission to medicine. Suddenly, this was another challenge between me and my goal, but I was determined. I remember the support of my friends in getting this done — specifically, Michael and other colleagues staying up overnight to help me revise and to encourage me to succeed.

I succeeded in getting an offer for the medicine 5-year programme. I opted for the full programme rather than the post-graduate 4-year programme because I did not want to do self-directed learning. The offer was conditional on me achieving a 2:1 in my biomedical science degree, but I got a 2:2. When I heard, I remember sitting down in tears in one of the rooms in university offices.

But it wasn't all over. My supervisor's had a meeting, and given how well I performed under the circumstances, the decision was made to grant me a place.

It would have been easy at any point in my illness to give up. With treatments, long admissions, pain, and uncertainty, I asked myself, "Why am I putting myself through this? For what purpose?" and I certainly could have given up. But life is about choosing to push through difficulties rather than settling for what's easier simply because it's convenient. Life doesn't offer easy paths, and what seems easy now won't necessarily stay that way. The easier road isn't always the better one. In fact, what you fight for—what you work tirelessly to achieve—becomes easier in the end because you've already fought for it.

Think about the old Viking days: the battle might be tough, but at the end, you celebrate the loot. Without struggle, there's no reward. If your journey is easy and the reward comes without effort, then congratulations. But for me, taking the harder path made me stronger. I know it's a cliché—"What doesn't kill you makes you stronger"—but I am undeniably stronger now. I'm not sure I'd be able to handle the challenges I face today without those prior hardships.

CHAPTER 6
DEALING WITH THE UNKNOWN

With my first illness, I was scared. The diagnosis was and remains unclear. I was not responding to any treatment. I had achieved my dream of admission to study medicine, but my own medical problems continued.

I was referred to Dr. Beverly Hunt at Kings who is one of the biggest hematologists in the country, and she did various tests and said "Look, I can't find anything. I don't know what this is, but it's not hematological." Initially, the provisional diagnosis of antiphospholipid syndrome had been considered, but my immune profile did not fit. Nothing fit really, so she sent me back to St. George's.

I was then sent to Professor Husker in Hammersmith, this

now being the third teaching hospital consulted. He admitted that he was at a loss and decided to put me on steroids (because that's what rheumatologists do). Lo and behold, I got better, and I stopped clotting. "So it is rheumatological syndrome," he said. I asked him which one, and he replied, "I don't know." Behçet's Syndrome had been mentioned several times, but again, I didn't fit the criteria for diagnosis. I continued to improve on the steroids and over time switched to Azathioprine and remained stable on this.

This unknown diagnosis made my getting any kind of insurance a nightmare. It became impossible to get travel insurance as I did not fit into their drop-down menus. My clinic letters mention diagnosis of Behçet's-like/Behçet's/possible Behçet's syndrome, whilst others stated "unknown autoimmune clotting disorder." The cost of life insurance was unbelievably high due to the uncertainty related to my diagnosis.

Over the course of 2 years, I spent 18 months in hospital. This was due to repeated infections in my leg, which required admission for surgical drainage as well as repeated courses of antibiotics, courses which became longer as the infections became more drug resistant. These were some of the hardest times. I was a young man in his early 20s who was suddenly bedbound in hospital. My asymmetric leg swelling became more obvious, but I got used to it.

My parents were worried throughout, and so I felt I had to be strong, to avoid worrying them. I had an amazing group of friends from my year at university who regularly visited me in hospital. Being older than most of them, I had mentored them. I knew they looked up to me, and I felt I had to be strong for them too. And I would be, every day, until visiting time was over. After the last person left, that's when I would cry, continuously for several hours and then go to sleep — every day.

Over time, I called it "the mask." It's dangerous because no one sees the real you. Some people wear these masks, and it can be off-putting. I've known people like that. When you dig deeper, you discover a completely different, beautiful, kind person beneath the mask. They wear it to protect themselves. I did the same, to maintain my image in front of my friends. I did it for my parents, too, because the more I broke, the more it hurt them. It taught me to try and look deeper in relationships and to try and see behind the mask that you may not realise a person wearing.

Looking back after those tough nights, however, I realize I didn't need to be so strong. My friends and family were there for me, and I didn't have to hide. Creating masks to protect myself or others isn't always the right choice. Now, with maturity, I see that if we don't support each other honestly, our relationships are built on false pretenses. Being open and real with each other is far more meaningful. I had so much support, then and now, and my journey back then may have been easier if I had leaned a little more into it. These lessons and experiences are helping me right now, because to attempt to deal with what I am going through now, alone, would be a fool's errand.

My brother Basil was my hero during this time period. The things I have put Basil through in this life, only God knows how he managed. He was in the monastery, a consecrated deacon, debating whether to enter into full-time ministry. He dropped everything to be by my bedside, day in and day out, without fail. He put his life on pause for those two years to be with me. I love my whole family, but what he did for me was incredible. I think that is why we are very, very close. It was not easy for him; those visits involved watching *Lord of the Rings*, the extended version, back-to-back over a day and a half on several occasions. It involved him helping with food, as there was no Uber Eats back then. I remember once he was a little bit resistant to going and buying food, and I explained that hospital food really shouldn't be for human consumption. He kept insisting I try something from the hospital, and he said that him providing a food delivery service was not sustainable.

I relented and said, "Okay. I'll order the rice pudding." When the rice pudding arrived, I told him, "Turn it upside down."

And he was like, "What?"

"Turn it upside down."

And he did. It was just stuck into the plate in a truly repulsive way. He responded, "I'll go get you something right now."

Bas was truly my guardian angel at this time. My whole family has had to endure the struggles and uncertainties of my illness with me, but none more than Bas, and I will be forever grateful to him.

On a side note, if my life were ever made into a film, I've always said there's only one man who could play me: Danny DeVito. Failing that, Tom Cruise, specifically, his character from *Tropic Thunder*. That character, with his over-the-top bravado and those wild dance moves at the end, that's me in a nutshell.

Speaking of acting, I did have my star moment in one of the plays at medical school. I usually did tech parts. However, in one revue, I choreographed and danced in a version of the "YMCA." I wore a skin-tight T-shirt and an old pair of tennis shorts from my GCSE days. The clothes, as you can imagine, were several sizes too small.

Somewhere in the chaos of the moment, I got a bit too into it and went interactive. I jumped off the stage, danced through the audience, found my good friend in the front row, and to his horror, gave him what can only be described as a surprise lap dance in front of a full auditorium. For weeks afterward, people kept coming up to me saying things like, "Wow. That was very convincing," often with raised eyebrows. Some were certain I wasn't acting. Looking back, it was probably one of the most ridiculous and unintentionally memorable occasions in medical school. Thank goodness this all happened just before mobile phones became the norm—there's no footage, and that's probably for the best.

CHAPTER 7
FIRST VISIT TO BELIZE

I knew I wanted to spend part of my medical elective in Canada. But I also knew that I wanted to spend time in South America and gain exposure to a different medical system. South America. was a region that intrigued me, filled with vibrant culture and diverse people. Naturally, I was drawn to the idea of immersing myself in the Spanish language. But the more I thought about it, the more I realized how challenging it would be to practice medicine in a language I was not fluent in. Although I took some lessons, progress was slow, and I realised I would not be at the level I needed to be fast enough. I then did a Google search for English-speaking South American countries, and Belize popped up. I had never even heard of Belize prior to this.

I found that Belize offered elective programs for students, though most were fairly expensive. As a student with a limited budget, that wasn't ideal, but after some digging, I realized I could arrange my own elective by contacting local hospitals directly. I shared my plan with my roommate and close friend, Kwok, and he was instantly interested in coming along. Honestly, I was relieved. The thought of going alone to a country I had never even heard of was daunting. So, we arranged the details, bought our flights, and embarked on our exciting adventure.

Our actual elective took place in Belize City. Though it is called Belize City, the capital of Belize had actually been moved to Belmopan due to the threat of hurricanes along the coast. Belize City, while bustling for its size, was still a small city compared to most capitals. The hospital where we worked wasn't the main one but was still central to the country's healthcare system. The doctors we met were knowledgeable and kind, but the hospital work wasn't overwhelming. We would arrive early in the morning, work for a few hours, and by lunchtime, we were often told there was nothing else to do, so we would leave and spend the rest of the day exploring.

We usually worked Monday through Thursday, and on Thursday evenings, we would board a coach to travel to one of the nearby coastal areas or to one of the islands. Belize has so much to offer. While many people only think of it as a stopover between Guatemala or Honduras, it had everything we needed to keep us entertained. The Caribbean coast offered pristine, white beaches, with turquoise waters and waving palm trees. At the time, Belize was not yet commercialized — no McDonald's or Burger Kings, just local independent businesses — which gave the country an authentic feel.

As well as beautiful coastlines, Belize also has one of the

densest rainforests in the world. It was easy to transition from beach relaxation to rainforest adventures, where we could explore caves, hike, zip line, or tubing down rivers. One of the highlights for me was visiting the ATM cave, an experience I will never forget. It was physically challenging, but it gave me the feeling of being Indiana Jones, swimming under rocks and jumping over obstacles in a cave that felt like something out of a movie. I did the cave twice—once during my elective and again later with Jen—and each time, it felt like an adventure in its purest form.

One of the things that truly captured my heart about Belize was the simplicity of the people. There's a sense of genuine happiness and helpfulness among the locals, and their openly faith-driven lifestyle resonated with me deeply. Whilst Belize City had a reputation for crime and all the shortcomings of most cities, including difficult people, absolutely everywhere else outside of the city felt safe and welcoming.

I came to realize that Belize wasn't just about its beauty or activities; it was about the people, the way of life, and the sense of peace I felt there. I felt more at home in Belize than I sometimes did in my own country. Despite the difference in culture, there was a fundamental overlap in values which made me feel deeply connected to the country. When I returned home after my elective, I found myself constantly talking about Belize until all my friends were completely fed up. I knew I had to return to Belize. It had given me so much during my time there, and I wanted to give something back.

CHAPTER 8
MORTGAGE, MEDICINE AND UNEXPECTED RETURNS

I always had an entrepreneurial mind. During my time at St George's, I needed somewhere to live and thought a house would be a good investment. I could live in one room and rent out the rooms, possibly even living in the house for free. I found the ideal house, a four-bedroom house on Pevensey Road, two minutes from the hospital. At the time, NatWest had a loan called the Graduate Guarantee Loan, which allowed me to raise the deposit needed. The house was bought in Ash and Bas's name because I didn't have a job, but it was fully financed by me, the deposit and mortgage. I was thrilled when it went through. It was a good investment, and to be a medical student on the housing ladder in your early 20s in London was quite an achievement.

I found tenants, though sometimes a room would be vacant, leaving me short on money. It brought worries, especially as a student juggling medicine, bills, a mortgage, and running things, even though the house was in my brothers' names. It involved a lot of work, but it was manageable. I was lucky to have good tenants, and I never had major issues. Later down the line, Jen became a tenant, and we began to get to know each other and eventually started dating.

The initial plan was to sell the house at the end of medical school and use the money to pay off my student loan, which after two degrees was sizeable. I consulted my brothers prior to doing this, who convinced me to keep it, citing rising property prices. I took their advice and kept the house. Three months later, Northern Rock Bank collapsed, and the property market crash followed. The house value dropped back to what I had paid for it. I couldn't rent it out because I wasn't near the university to find students. A year went by, and I was struggling to pay the mortgage and my normal rent. Then, out of desperation, someone introduced me to an estate agent who promised to fill the house in a week. At the time, I was asking for £1,000 in rent, but he managed to get £600. I was under huge financial pressure, so I reluctantly accepted. The tenants turned out to be vile. They destroyed the house and eventually stopped paying rent. Evicting them proved a nightmare, with court proceedings and bailiffs before we could remove them. When the bailiff went inside, he took a few steps, came out, and said, "It's bad, but I've seen worse." He went back in, came out again, and said, "No, I've never seen anything like this." Furniture was broken, and there were holes in the wall and unidentified marks everywhere. I didn't know what to do. Fix? Sell? It was hard, but I decided to sell.

It was heartbreaking to see the state it was in. I had so many amazing memories there. It became the unofficial social bar, where we would meet prior to going out. There had been numerous house parties, movie nights, and karaoke nights. Some of the best memories from medical school were in that house. It was difficult to give it up, but the situation with the tenants had been so painful that it was a relief to say, "This ordeal is over." But then, if I didn't have the house, I wouldn't have met Jen, and that alone makes it worth it. Every penny, every heartache, everything was worth it because I gained so much more.

CHAPTER 9
RETURN TO BELIZE

After I finished medical school and started my work as a junior doctor, my life became pretty busy. There was the reality of paying off student loans, and as much as I wanted to, I couldn't afford to visit Belize for a while. The flights were expensive, and though living there was cheap, the travel costs to get to the States to then reach Belize were prohibitive. Although life moved on and I got married to Jen, the idea of going back to Belize still lingered. Jen hadn't been before, but she had heard me go on and on about Belize and so she was not too difficult to convince. She liked the idea and, as always, lent her unconditional support.

We both felt in our current stage of training we would be in a good position to give back. At the time, healthcare in Belize was poor. They had a national health service, but the system was struggling. Belize had once been British Honduras before becoming Belize in 1981, the very year I was born. It felt symbolic that Belize and I shared the same birth year.

We made plans to go and set up a charity called Royal Blue Egg (RBE) to facilitate the process. RBE was named because we thought the globe looked like a blue egg, and it's our home, and it looks after us, so it's royal. That's how RBE was born, with the support of my brother and my sister-in-law. It is still a charity that exists to this day, although not as active as it used to be.

We started to contact hospitals to identify needs, and we decided to go more rural, so we could have more of an impact. At the time, my background was respiratory, so my plan was to run an asthma clinic. Jen was a surgical trainee, so she would support in that capacity. We started fundraising to allow us to buy equipment. We knew for us, our own expenses would be out of pocket, but we wanted to take simple things like pulse oximeters, blood glucose machines, and blood pressure machines with us. I also remembered from my previous visit that there was no antenatal scanning program, since there was no ultrasound machine. The only way to get antenatal scans was to pay privately, so we decided this was something we would also bring.

We held several functions to raise money. We did cheese and wine tastings, a Christmas ball, auctions, and a raffle. We tried to raise as much money as we could. Through this, the generosity of companies, hospitals, friends and family we managed to raise enough to purchase all the equipment we needed, including the ultrasound machine. The actual cost of the machine in the UK was too high, so I had one from China shipped straight to Belize. It was not fancy, but for antenatal scanning, it was sufficient.

The hospital we had chosen was in Dangriga. The plan was initially for me to provide respiratory care, but we soon realized respiratory is not what they needed. They needed diabetic care. At the time, the number one cause of death was complication of diabetes. It was a very difficult one to treat over there because people ate what they could afford. What they could afford was the mashed potato, the fried plantain. They could not afford meat, so the dinner plate was three carbs and a small bit of protein. You could not tell them not to eat it because they could not afford an alternative; it was a diabetes of necessity. It took me a while working with what they had in order to come up with a diet that patients would actually eat.

The other problem was the availability of drugs. Unlike in the UK, where there are so many options for treatment you lose track of what is available, in Belize, I only had the option of two drugs: insulin and metformin. The insulin was old school, drawn out of a glass jar. The other drug, metformin, we soon discovered varied in dosage. A pharmacist who was working there explained to us that whilst she was working in the main hospital, she noted that the people on metformin issued by the hospital pharmacy were struggling to control their sugars. However, whenever a relative sent them medication of the same dose from the USA, their blood sugars were better controlled. She investigated further and had the metformin tablets analysed, and found out that the active ingredient in the hospital issued drug was only 7%. When she raised the alarm, she was essentially exiled to our hospital. Facts like these created huge challenges in prescribing effective treatment. Thus, I decided to focus on what I could control: education. There was almost no public education on diabetes in Belize, so we worked to raise awareness. We held community events, went on the radio, and designed a diet plan to help manage diabetes. It was incredible to see the impact, even though I wasn't there long enough to gather comprehensive data. We partnered with a local pharmacy and managed to track HbA1c levels, and the positive results from the education and dietary changes felt really rewarding. I remember, one woman, in her seventies, took three buses to see me, saying she wanted to be there because she needed to come and see me. We even set up a local diabetic association and invited people from the community to get involved. I helped organize talks and brought in a podiatrist for foot care education. The first meeting was one of my proudest moments and is a memory which I treasure.

It's moments like these when I truly believe that there is a plan for everything. Prior to coming to Belize, as I had stepped out of training to arrange the trip, I had 4 months free. Believe it or not, the job I had for those four months was in diabetes. It turned out to be the perfect preparation. Thankfully, I had strong connections with my consultants back home as well and was able to reach out to them whenever I faced a tricky situation or wasn't sure how to proceed.

When I first made plans to go to Belize with Jen, I had hoped to bring along some consultants to make a bigger impact. I reached out to a few who showed interest, and we had several discussions with the management about logistics, including pay, whether the positions would be voluntary, and if the UK hospitals would contribute to the consultants' salaries. Unfortunately, it became complicated, with too many moving parts to work out. Things became even more challenging when a show by Ross Kemp aired about the most dangerous cities in the world. One of the episodes focused on Belize City, and after it aired, a few of the consultants who had initially agreed to join us began backing out. They'd seen the show and understandably had second thoughts. They started saying, "Sorry. I'm okay. I'm out." Although we didn't take any consultants, we did manage to take another junior doctor and four elective students. This arrangement helped with finances, as we were able to share the costs of accommodation and other expenses, essential given that we were living off our savings.

There were definitely a lot of frustrating moments. One of the biggest hurdles was the hospital management's attitude. They were used to the large American NGOs that would come in and set up temporary clinics and function independently. We wanted to work differently by setting up sustainable projects. We didn't want to be one of the groups that gave new tablets for a month and left, with no consideration for the patient's ongoing care. What frustrated me even more was the culture of dependency. Whenever I asked the hospital to help us with something, the answer was almost always, "Go to your NGO." But there was no NGO; there were just two of us, living out of pocket, trying to make a difference. I think the management had become so accustomed to the idea of outside aid that they couldn't fathom someone doing it without financial backing from a large organization.

We even tried to work with the Ministry of Health to streamline the process and make things easier, like purchasing equipment directly through them. But we soon learned that the government was paying five or six times the price for items compared to what we could get. The middlemen involved in the process were taking a cut at every stage, and it was frustrating to see how inefficient and corrupt the system was. Even when we got the equipment in, getting it out of customs was a nightmare. I refused to pay a "brown envelope" fee for the customs to release the items. I refused to use donated money for this purpose. Eventually, after pushing and pushing, we got everything out, but it took a lot longer than it should have.

The most frustrating moment came when we finally got the ultrasound machine that we had raised funds for. I had told the hospital that I wanted people there to receive it, so we could take pictures and show the donors the impact of their generosity. But when I called ahead to check that the relevant people would be available, I was told there was no one to receive it. I called the Ministry of Health contact I had, and he told me I could give the machine to another hospital. So, instead of handing it over to the ungrateful team at the first hospital, we took it to the staff at Belmopan, where I knew they would appreciate it. The doctors there were so much more welcoming and receptive. The chief of staff took pictures with us, and they immediately started using the machine. The next day, the first hospital was furious. They didn't understand why I had given the machine away. But I explained that they had shown no interest, so why should I leave it with them? The staff at Belmopan had shown far more appreciation than the hospital we were supposed to be working with.

Financially, the situation was getting more difficult as time went on. By January, we were barely scraping by—living off the bare minimum, still paying student loans, and facing daily challenges just to make ends meet. But somehow, we made it through. It was a tough four months, but I'm glad we did it. The struggles were many, but the experience was worth it.

The happy memories we have would fill a book in its own right. Outside the hospital, life was every bit as heavenly as when I visited the first time. In that time, the infrastructure had become a bit more commercial, especially on the islands. There were larger hotels with more rooms and concrete structures instead of the quaint, smaller places we'd initially seen. Though it lost a bit of its charm with the increased commercialisation, the warmth and kindness of the people remained.

Our house in Dangriga, was absolutely beautiful—two floors, right on the beach. The view was breathtaking, with the sea right outside our door. We had two hammocks where we would relax after work, enjoying a cold beer, watching the ocean, and reflecting on the day. We walked to and from the hospital; it was about a 25-minute walk. I think by the end of the trip I was probably the healthiest and slimmest I've ever been. Our walks were usually punctuated by multiple conversations with the locals who were often cooking outside and would insist on sharing their food with us. They didn't expect anything in return. It was their way of saying thank you for the work we were doing.

A favourite place we found whilst we there was called "The Shack." It was located by a small estuary, where local fishermen would bring in their fresh catches. We'd often go there to buy freshly caught fish, which we'd then take home and grill ourselves. But the shack itself was our go-to spot for dinner in the evenings. It was tiny, just three tables in a wooden hut, no more than 4x4 meters in size, with a tiny kitchen and just one burner. It was run by a husband and wife, and we ate there regularly. The menu was always the same: premade fajitas. A few nights a week, there was a guy playing the piano, and we made sure to be there when he was performing. It was always the same songs, and "Ring of Fire" was always one of them. Together, though, it was perfection. It wasn't fine dining, but the combination of atmosphere, scenery, evening breeze, and a cold beer made it perfect in its own way.

I think Belize will always have a special place in my heart. Unfortunately, not being able to go back has been hard. We were waiting for Luke to get old enough to have his vaccines and be able to swim. When he did, Sophia arrived. Jen fell in love with it too. It will always be our special place.

CHAPTER 10
FROM SCRUBS TO GELATO... AND BACK AGAIN.

I spent years seeing the NHS change in ways that frustrated me, feeling like patient care was losing its focus. But my desire for a new challenge had been burning inside me for a long time. Even during my medical training, I had always ideas of opening a bar. I enjoyed hosting and socialising, and was well known for my cocktail making skills! Jen and I talked many times about opening a restaurant. Initially as an idea, then eventually seriously, I thought it could be a good business that could set up my family financially. Medicine was my passion, but the idea of owning and running my own place became the pull I needed to step away from medicine for a while.

The inspiration for the setup came from Belize. During our time there, Jen and I discovered a small gelato shop run by an Italian-French couple in a town called Palencia. Their gelato was incredible, made with fresh, local fruit. We used to buy the ice cream and go sit under a palm tree, in front of the beach, enjoying the flavours and talking. These were some of our best memories. They also served incredible food, mango salsa, jerk chicken, tastes so incredible that we brought everyone who visited us to try. I knew that somehow I wanted to recreate that experience in this venture.

Recognising it was my dream, Jen stood by me, always supportive. She is a pragmatic person, and I could see her thinking that I was completely crazy, but she was with me all the way. She saw my passion and matched it always. If I put 120%, she would meet me with the same. She has been my cheerleader from day one. There is something about having a person that supports you in everything that makes you believe you can do anything. So with this new plan, we decided that 2015 would be the year to open our business.

We knew having a restaurant would take some time to organise so we decided to start with creating and selling Gelato. We felt there was a market for this. We were close enough to the coast to have a lot of tourists passing through, but there was no high-quality ice cream
establishment in the area. I took it seriously and decided to master the craft; to fully recreate a true paradise experience, I knew the product had to be good. I signed up to the Gelato University in Italy and undertook the courses required to become a certified Gelato Chef.

The next challenge was the location. We found a place that was just within budget, but slightly off the public footfall. It was a garden square just behind the main shopping high street. At the same time, the council released plans to redo this square into a food hub, with TV screens and outdoor seating areas. We felt we would fit well into this outlook. The unit was large, two floors, with separate entrances, ideal for my vision of running a day-to-night operation. But it was in desperate need of TLC. I had faith in the council's plans to transform the area into a bustling food hub, and so did our investors. The idea was simple, secure a low rent now, and when the area developed, we would already be in a prime spot at a fraction of the cost. Jen and I signed the lease.

Jen had just given birth to our son, Luke, in January 2015, and by August of the same year, we were opening the shop. The week prior to the opening was a whirlwind of activity. Friends and family came down and stayed with us to paint, clean, set up, and prepare for the opening. There were inevitable glitches along the way, including the grand opening. On the big day, the machine broke down, and we were unable to serve gelato until the end of the day. Not the start we envisaged, but we persevered.

After the rocky start, things initially went well. We became well known in the area and had regulars. We then moved to open the restaurant side of the business that I headed.

Unfortunately, the redevelopment of the square that we were promised never materialised. We had gone big, perhaps too big, importing custom-made counters from Italy that I designed myself and installing high-end marble finishes, because I was convinced that the
market was there, so I went all out. Although we had our

regulars, most of the tourist traffic that we were targeting never passed through, despite us taking samples to the high street to convince people to make the small detour. The weather didn't always cooperate either. After all, this was Wales, and the low season was a lot longer than the high season. It was difficult, but after several years of challenging times, we made the decision to close.

For me, the journey wasn't just about creating a business, it was about pursuing my passion. It was about challenging myself and proving that I could make something work, even in the face of uncertainty. Looking back on the journey today, I feel a deep sense of accomplishment. Our gelato shop was more than just a business, it's a testament to my willingness to step outside my comfort zone, to continuously challenge myself.

Medicine was always my passion, but I had to step away from training whilst setting up the business. My plan was always to return to medicine once the business was running. This time away did rekindle my passion for my job, and I re-embarked on my career with new spirit.

It was not an easy time for my family because I had spent long hours invested in the business. I feel blessed to have had Jen by my side, as my soulmate and life partner. She has understood and supported the pursuit of my dreams. It is because of her I feel fulfilled today and that I've accomplished all that I need to. I truly don't know where I would be without her love and unwavering support.

CHAPTER 11
KNOW THYSELF

There are three types of people: the problem-maker, the problem-identifier, and the problem-solver. The problem-maker is easy to understand; they do exactly that, so we do not need to talk more about them. The problem-identifier is normally viewed negatively. These are the people who see the complication in everything: "Let's do this" is followed by "Oh no. We can't because X or Y might happen." They can be irritating. But slowly you see that this is a talent. I call myself a problem-solver, but often I don't see the problem to solve it! Jen is a problem-identifier. It's why Jen and I work really well as a team. There is a little bit of overlap in the two characteristics for sure, but most people are usually more of one than the other. In my experience, healthy relationships result from when a combination of the two work well together. The last thing you need are two problem identifiers, on a project or in life, because then the situation is definitely not going anywhere. Conversely, two problem solvers and the project may reach dizzy heights before collapsing spectacularly.

If you identify yourself as a problem-identifier, awareness of this trait will help you know when to tone it down. Yes, you need to illustrate the problem, but not of every little thing that could go wrong. If you're a problem solver, it can be hard, because once people see you as such, they are more likely to consistently approach you with issues, and it can get overwhelming. I am more appreciative of problem identifiers since being with Jen. It's not that they see the bad in everything, but it's because they are genuinely concerned. Harnessing their insight can make for very successful ventures. Seeing the traits in your friends and partners can help you work together more harmoniously.

CHAPTER 12
THE SECOND ILLNESS

Jen and I went on a cruise at the beginning of December 2023 to celebrate Jen's 40th. We came back just before Christmas and spent Christmas with my parents. Nothing out of the ordinary. After New Year's, I started with a bad cough and a cold. My blood tests were fine except for low platelets, which I didn't make much of. At the time, I was admitting so many patients with parainfluenza, influenza, COVID, or RSV, so I assumed it was all viral. However, I would get slightly better than worse again, never quite recovering.

In February 2024, I was admitted with sepsis, but the swab showed parainfluenza. It was assumed that I was running this course because I was immunosuppressed. I was discharged after 2 days but still did not feel 100%.

Before we went on the cruise, we had a positive pregnancy test. Jen had a coil in, but it was not visible when she went for her scan. She had several further scans, which were all inconclusive, until the one just before we set off, which suggested Jen was pregnant. So we went on the cruise thinking we were pregnant. Jen didn't drink and followed all the rules, which was tough because she had been researching this cruise and planned the celebration for so long. When we came back, our repeat scan showed there was a sac but no viable pregnancy. Although it wasn't a planned pregnancy, the result did affect us — Jen more than me. She went home after the scan, and I went back to work. I remember being at work that day and trying to concentrate and realising that I just couldn't; I was worried about Jen and realised I needed to be with her. I let HR know that I was going home due to personal reasons and left.

After this emotional day, I was still feeling unwell and took a further two days of sick leave. On the second day of my sick leave, I went to Luke's nativity play. Unfortunately, word of this reached my workplace, and upon returning, I found myself having to explain it. After 14 years of dedicated service, it was disheartening to feel that my integrity might be in question. So despite being unwell in January and February, I struggled through and continued to attend work.

Following my discharge, I started experiencing high fevers again, >40 °Celsius, repeatedly. I was readmitted, and it was still considered to be infective, possibly tropical given my recent travel. We consulted the London School of Hygiene and Tropical Medicine. They were not convinced but agreed to do tests. I felt like Mel Gibson in *Braveheart* because the tests they were doing were sent to specialized labs across the UK. So, I think there's a bit of my blood everywhere in the

UK at the moment.

Everything kept coming back negative for infection, no positive cultures and nothing on the CT scans. I was on several different antibiotics, bleach therapy essentially. Apart from the fever, I had no other symptoms. Platelets kept being low, which we assumed was because of consumption-inflammation or infection was causing my platelets to be used up faster than my body was producing them.

Given my background and the fact that all microbiology was clear, a rheumatological condition was raised, possibly Hemophagocytic Lymphohistiocytosis (HLH). This had four predisposing factors: use of drugs, such as azathioprine; autoimmune disease; genetics (which present earlier in life); and lymphoproliferative. The first two factors applied in my case so an opinion was sought from the specialist team in London, and they recommended steroids. As I had the bone marrow analysis and PET CT pending, my doctors chose to hold administering the steroids until they were performed.

The consultants on the respiratory team, which were essentially my parent team, were awesome. They were the main team directing my care and liaising with other specialties. The nurse that escorted me for my PET CT had instructions to give me steroids the minute I came off the table. And lo and behold, as soon as I had that 40 mg dose, the fever came down. Up until that point, it had been resistant to everything. I spent the day drenched in sweat, with no concern for dignity, wearing only boxers with a fan pointed at me and a wet flannel on my head.

After I had the bone marrow, the respiratory consultant came to me direct: "Look, George, you have contacts everywhere in this hospital. Some of the results are back. And I don't want you to just hear it in passing from someone. I think it's looking like a lymphoma." I thought of my mum having lymphoma, now in remission and thought, "Okay, I can manage this." I called my family and Basil got on a flight.

In the meantime, the rheumatology team was still thinking an autoimmune process required exclusion, as they hadn't seen part of the bone marrow results. They wanted to run more tests, including MR and CT, and came in to let me know as such. Jen was with me, and together we were thinking, "Maybe things aren't so bad here. This is good news. It's not malignant. It's autoimmune."

But an hour and a half later, our world was turned upside down. The hematologist walked in and said, "Sorry, George. There's been a lot of confusion about what's been happening. But I think we've finally managed to put everything together. We have discussed it with Cardiff lymphoma team and it is lymphoma. Not only is it lymphoma, but it's T-cell lymphoma. Not only is it a T-cell lymphoma, ut it's a hepatosplenic T cell."

"Okay," I responded, "What does that mean?"

"It's a very rare, very aggressive lymphoma. And your bone marrow shows a quite extensively active disease. We want to consent you for chemotherapy and get it started ASAP — really."

Jen and I were paralysed. Just as I was coming to terms with having a lymphoma, to be told and hour and half ago that it's not lymphoma and it's auto immune, to now being told it is the most aggressive lymphoma, and I was already Stage 4. Within 10 minutes, the whole family was in the room, which made the whole thing even more overwhelming.

The medical team were keen to discharge me. I was fever free and due to start chemotherapy the following week. Two days following my discharge, I started having palpitations. A pulse check revealed a heart rate of 200 beats per minute. I was in fast atrial fibrillation. Following trials of metoprolol in resuscitation, I ended up needing cardioversion, which thankfully was successful, and I was able to start chemotherapy two days later.

I did my own research, but given the complexity of my case, I was also discussed with London and Oxford specialist centres. A regime called IVAC was recommended with a scan after two cycles. The follow-up scan showed my disease had progressed in the spleen. I had a repeat bone marrow performed, which showed increased disease activity in the marrow. The advice from London was to stop treatment and switch to palliation.

Unfortunately, my hematology doctor in Cardiff couldn't meet me that day in the clinic, so it was a new doctor who got the short straw to break that news to me. She was quite honest in the prognosis being really poor and the first one that said "months." I'd say that was quite a lot to take in then. That was a hard day. But after discussion, we agreed that we were going to finish the four cycles.

It was actually my rheumatologist here in Carmarthen who then raised the immunotherapy as a trial. Even with limited research, she said, "It works in Hodgkin's. It works in B-cell, in some cases. I haven't really tried it in T-cell. Very limited trials in T-cell. But what do we have to lose?" And I agreed. I fully agreed. It needed to apply for funding because it's outside the remit. The general consensus was that the chances are it would not work. But again, I had nothing to lose.

In the ideal situation, the scans would have shown that I had gone into remission after the second cycle. I would then have a bone marrow transplant which would be potentially curative. In this type of lymphoma, the research is limited, with only 200 published cases. The paper in the IVAC chemotherapy that was given to me only had 14 people. In the medical world, these are very small cohorts, but all the papers showed that the transplant could be curative. Prior to this stage, both Ash and Bas had tested to be potential donors, and thankfully, Ash was a match. Not only was he a match, but a very good match. This would mean the risks of complications, such as graft versus host, were significantly reduced. This was excellent news at the time because being of non-Caucasian descent, the bone marrow registry would have been unlikely to have found a match for me. Unfortunately, despite this potential good news, my disease progression did not allow this to be an option.

CHAPTER 13
BETWEEN HOPE AND SURRENDER

The experience has been an emotional rollercoaster. At first, when I was admitted, there wasn't much emotion because I thought it was an infection, something we could treat easily. Then, when it was H&H, I assumed steroids or a similar treatment would fix things, so I kept my emotions in check. But when I was finally diagnosed, that's when the emotions hit. I understood chemotherapy and the life changes it would bring, so I started processing it. There was a brief high when it seemed not to be the case, but then a huge emotional hit came after, when I realized the prognosis and began fully understanding the disease.

There was no fear. I wasn't afraid. I think I was just sad. I automatically went into worry mode and tried to sort out the finances, then tried to sort life out, because sorting became something I could do, something I could control. I couldn't control the sadness, and I couldn't control the disease. All I could do was focus on everything else other than the disease.

It has been difficult to have alone time with Jen. We read the Bible every day together, a Psalm, a chapter of St. John, just to help me focus on things. My constant prayer was asking God to just make it work: "You don't give us more than we can bear. You've done this 24 years ago, and you've seen me through it. This is another one. It's more challenging, but you've done the first one so well, that this one should be okay."

Initially, the plan was clear. A 30% five-year survival rate wasn't great, but we could be optimistic. All I had to do was focus on the chemotherapy. I think I tried to keep that optimism, but when we had the news confirming disease progression and that prognosis was months, things came into more focus. That day was just something else. They gave us an office, and Jen and I cried. We just kept crying and crying and crying. Ash was there, so they called him up and told him what was happening. He was crying as well. I still had to go through cycle 3, and Jen had to drive back to Carmarthen alone.

From then, there was a lot of begging, and saying, "Look, I can't. I have my family I know You have Your plan, but I just can't. I don't want to leave my family." And sometimes, up to now, my prayer is always divided: "Look, I want to accept Your will, because it got me here. Your plan got me here, through thick and thin, I want to accept it" but then, on the other side, I pray, "I want to get better, and I don't know if Your plan is for me to get better or not, but if it isn't for me to get better, then I beg for more time with my family."

With the kids, it's been difficult, because the more fun I have with them, the more sad I become, because I'm more aware of what I'm going to be missing, so I'll do something with them, and outside I'll be laughing with them, but inside I'll be breaking because I'm acutely aware that this is what I'm going to miss, which is quite difficult.

Hiding the implications from the family was tricky. When I received the diagnosis, Bas was on the plane within 6 hours. Again, he has dropped everything to be at my side, together with Joyce. He's helping with everything — logistics, finances, family communications, sparing me from the burden. Just like he did all those years ago. When we told my parents, we did it in the hospital, just in case it was too much and they needed medical attention. I think they had a clue what was coming, with Bas flying out at the last minute and me starting to write a book. Mum is always praying for me, and there's always something they send me — an oil or sand or a relic.

I have a relic of Saint Mina, part of his garment, which is normally only kept in churches, in my house. The situation is such that when Abouna came and was like, "My oil. I didn't realize it's finished."

We were all like, "Don't you worry. Which oil do you want? Who do you want? Which monastery? Which saint? Which geographical state do you want?" Thanks to mum, I have a bag full of oils, waters, sands, enough to bless the whole country, I think.

We try to laugh. I can see everyone is worried about me. I can see their pain. In the middle of the day, we sometimes forget what's happening. None of this has been easy, and I still do not understand. But I know that I have been blessed with so much. My focus is to give as much love to my family as possible and fill whatever moments I have with them with happiness.

CHAPTER 14
TELLING LUKE

The hardest part for me during my second illness was seeing how it affected my children. With Sophia, it wasn't possible to explain anything because she was so young, but with Luke, we had to have a conversation fairly early on about what was going on. At the start, we told him I was sick and that I might have to go in and out of the hospital for treatment. He took it well and showed a lot of maturity. He did show signs of emotional strain, like occasional outbursts or moments when he lacked patience, but considering everything, he handled it well.

Initially, he used to come to visit me in the hospital, but as time went by, he didn't want to see me in the hospital. He'd ask questions from time to time, such as how I was doing and if I was getting better. I'd explain that we were trying different treatments, and he seemed to accept it without many questions. He didn't have lots of questions; he just got on with it. Sometimes, he didn't understand quite why I was not there as much.

When I'm at home, we usually have what I call our boys' morning, where me and him will go downstairs before Jen and Sophia just to play on the PlayStation and have breakfast together. More recently, it's our hot chocolate time, because it's a bit cold as well. It's our time together, and I think that it is quite important to him because he gets dedicated time with me. One morning, though, I didn't feel well, and as I started explaining that my illness was proving harder to treat, and we both got a little teary. I told him how much I hated not being able to spend more time with him. He was emotional but understanding.

Jen and I debated when the right time would be to tell him the full story and the futility of it all. We waited because we didn't want it to affect his school, but Jen felt it was important to tell him soon, with all the visitors coming and going. I think he'd already picked something was going on. That day, just as we were still debating whether it was the right time, Luke came downstairs after his bath and said, "Dad, I have a few questions." My assumption was that it was going to be football related, but his question was, "I wanted to ask about your medication."

At that point, I realized it was the right time to talk. Jen wasn't there yet, so I began explaining that the first medication we had tried hadn't worked and that we were going to try a different one, but we weren't sure if it would help. I told him that it seemed like I might stay sick for longer. When Jen came downstairs, we continued the conversation. I explained that if this new treatment doesn't work—there's only a small chance it might—then I would keep getting sicker, and it might mean I won't be around anymore.

He asked, "What does that mean, 'not here anymore'?" I think he understood more than we expected, even though Jen and I had tried to avoid using words like "dying." Eventually, I believe he figured it out on his own. His response was unexpectedly mature and thoughtful. The first thing he said was, "I'm sorry you're going through this." It showed a level of maturity I hadn't anticipated from him. He then followed with "It's okay because Jesus is on our side." That made me really proud because I had always felt a bit guilty, thinking I wasn't doing enough in terms of teaching him about religion. We pray every night and say grace before meals, but sometimes I feel like I could do more, such as share more Bible stories with him. He spoke about the importance of family and sticking together, and it sounded so much like me. At the end, he said, "We'll stick together because that's what families do. We stick together. Jesus will help us as much as He can."

I thought to myself, how mature for a nine-year-old to respond like that! It gave me a huge sense of comfort, knowing there's a strong foundation there for him to grow into a good man. Jen and I have done a good job. I don't need to worry about them so much because I know the foundation is solid. I trust and have faith that he will grow up with a strong sense of values, becoming an incredible person. It's not just because of what I've taught him so far, but also because of what Jen will continue to teach him.

I explained to him the purpose of the book—though I might not be there to help him, the book would be his way of getting to know me more. I told him, "This book is for you and your sister. It shows you who I was. You got to know me more than she did, but this book is for both of you to understand who I am." He then went upstairs with Jen. He cried, but he told Jen that they would help each other and support each other. For me, yes, I felt incredible sadness that I would miss part of their lives, but it gives me comfort knowing that they are together and that they will be okay.

CHAPTER 15

HE WHO HAS A BROTHER

My two brothers are everything to me. We grew up as best friends. They have over and over again moved heaven and earth for me. The minute I say, "I need you," they're there. They drop everything; they're there. They've been my protectors, my greatest supporters, my greatest motivators, and my role models. They are both two completely different characters, and I have learnt so much from both. I cannot imagine my life without them.

I would love for Luke and Sophia to treasure each other as I treasure my brothers. In family, you have everything. If you have a brother or sister, they are your blood, your family. And when they need you, or you need them, they will be there. The moment you need them, they'll show up. You'll have friends, even best friends, and sometimes they'll come when you need them, but sometimes they won't. With family, though, your brother will come, or your sister will come. Likewise, you'll go to them if they need you. Treasure your family, and always put God and family before anything else.

There are times when you will feel alone. Don't be scared to reach out. When you keep a problem to yourself, it just spirals and festers inside you, and it makes the problem worse rather than better. Don't distance yourself from the people who are trying to help you. My advice is that if you ever find yourself alone, don't be too proud, and don't be too afraid to look around and ask for help.

My dear Luke and Sophia, you will always have help. Look at the family you have been born to, and you will see that you are surrounded by people who love you. If you ever struggle, call them. You will quickly realize that you were silly to begin to feel alone because you are so, so loved. I keep repeating this, but its who I am. For me, God and family are the two most important things in my life, and then medicine. God and family, by far — everything else doesn't matter.

CHAPTER 16
MY FAITH, MY RELIGION

My religion and the Church were foundational in my life and have been integral to my development as a person. As a child, I grew up in the Church, and it was a constant presence in my life. We were always there, not just on Sundays, but even during the week. There were always activities and things going on. There was not as much available for me compared to Basil and Ash, who were heavily involved, but I participated in whatever was available to me, such as listening to the Bible stories and lessons from them. Looking back, one of my regrets is not involving my own kids in church more as they were growing up. I think I've fallen short in that area, and Jen has been the one to focus more on that. I do wish did more to ensure they had a stronger connection to church, especially since it played such a huge role in shaping who I am today. I hope they can take something from these stories.

It wasn't until my teenage years that I really began to practice what I had learned, rather than just listening and absorbing. There was one moment that I realised as a teenager it had become more. We used to go to these conferences, and I don't know what age that would be, mid-teens maybe. We had a prayer time ,and suddenly I started praying out loud, and I prayed for quite a bit. Then after, everyone just came up to me and said,
"We found it very moving." I don't know what triggered it, but something was different in me from that day.

Through my life, the way I practiced my religion was slightly different from the rest of the family. For example, my brother Ash is more old-school, believing that you need to read your Bible everyday and go to church every Sunday. Whereas for me, it's more emotional. Until this day, I always have a cross in my pocket. I don't go to church every Sunday, and I rarely read the Bible. People who work with me may not know that I'm a Christian. My relationship with God is more personal and constant. I reach for Him and reach for my cross. Whenever I go through a difficult moment, I put my hand in my pocket hold my cross and repeat: You're my comfort, you're my strength, you get me through this, and that's it. I don't need to make a big deal about it. I don't need to because it's a continuous relationship. He's ever-present. He's ever there, and I don't need to book an appointment. That's my relationship. I believe in the sacraments of the Church, I participate in communion, even though I don't have as much communion as I should. I probably definitely don't confess as much as I should, and I think that is important also. But I also think we can sometimes regiment religion into life, which makes it lose meaning for me.

My relationship with God is simple and, in many ways, aligns with the New Testament view of God. My cross is my link to Him. I hold my cross, I say two or three lines that apply to that moment that I need him, or even I start a project at work and say, "Just help me get through this." If I am slightly angry at someone, I'll say ,"Help me process this." It really is a friendship. I'm not saying everyone should do it exactly the way I do because that might not work for them. I think this works for me. It's the way I am able to live and practice my faith.

How does that line up with what I have experienced in my life and my struggles? During my first illness, I spent a lot of time in the hospital. I had a lot of time to think. I was angry that it had happened to me at that time. I couldn't understand why all this would happen in my final, most important year of school. I kept asking God, "Why? Why don't you want me to be a doctor? Why don't you want me to do this? Why now? Why like this?" I just could not understand it. But in the midst of it, you remember how small we are. Who are we to ask why? Can you fit an ocean in a cup of water? All we see just is right now, right here. We don't understand the bigger picture, the bigger plan, what's in store.

When I look back, I can see the greater plan. Those two years where I spent 18 months in hospital, the majority of them were the first two years of medicine that were identical to the first year of biomedicine. That meant despite being 18 months in hospital, I didn't have to take time off the course, and I could continue, since I already knew the material. I was just able to come down as inpatient and do my exams and go back to the ward. I remember going to the end of year OSCEs with my patient wristband, and the examiner thought it was a dare or a sick joke. I had to say, "No, I'm genuinely a patient on the ward." Before one of my exams, one of the consultants in charge of my care actually did a revision session with me, helping me practice how to examine reflexes before I went downstairs for the exam!

Obviously, I didn't want to be ill, and it was a struggle to understand why I was, but given the circumstances, the only way that this timeline of my degree would have worked was like this. I became ill, but things worked so that I could still carry on and achieve my dream of being a doctor despite that. I managed to complete 2 years without attending lectures. So then you see that this can't be by chance, and this can't be by coincidence. There's a higher power here who looks at the whole picture.

I think it gave me a greater love and understanding, to not question the path or why. Because suddenly, I look back at that time I was asking why, and I'm like, "Well, there you go. You have your answer now, don't you?" And I think that tells me now, not to question why, but to accept the plan. It doesn't make sense to me now either, but who am I? I have to accept it. No one knows what else could have happened. If I didn't have this sickness, I mean, what would the future have held? For example, I could have been in a road traffic collision and paraplegic. I don't know.

When I was diagnosed earlier this year, everyone was just telling me, "Don't be scared, don't be scared, don't be scared." And I was able to say I am not. Last time, I was a young kid, I was scared. This time, I am not scared at all, one bit. I've achieved my dreams in medicine. But I also had dreams as a parent. I wanted to see my children graduate, walk my daughter down the aisle, and see them have their children. It's hard coming to terms with the fact that this is not going to happen. I am happy for the part of their lives I have been able to share and hope they can share in my life through this book.

CHAPTER 17

MESSAGES FOR A DISCONNECTED WORLD.

One outcome I didn't like from the COVID-19 pandemic is that it made people more distant. Even before the pandemic, we were drifting apart due to our obsession with phones. Even if you sit in a room with people, everyone is on their phone. We're more likely to message someone or Instagram someone or anything than to make an effort to actually speak to that person, call them, or even meet them. The pandemic made this worse because we became more dependent on the phone and remote communication rather than talk face to face. And some places have stayed that way (e.g. multidisciplinary meetings), which has some benefits, but at the end of the day, a lot of social interaction with your work colleagues has disappeared; each little interaction builds connections and help us to grow relationships. Virtual meetings have become the default, meetings being held over Microsoft Teams, even when we could meet in person and speak face to face. It makes interactions feel distant and impersonal. I miss those spontaneous connections.

It is the same thing with birthdays now. I'm old because I mention Facebook. Although the birthday reminder is great, it feels so impersonal. I know it's easy and quick, but I try to make an effort to send a text or even call someone on their birthday. It's just a small gesture, but it shows that you care and value the person, rather than just clicking through an automatic reminder.

Let's not depend so much on our technologies to communicate with each other and actually take the time to speak to each other and meet face to face and have that social interaction. If you can have a meeting, we say, "Guys, let's not just do Teams this time. Let's just actually meet like we used to and have a meeting and face to face." I truly believe we get so much more accomplished when we connect face to face. It's more personal, more effective, and helps us build stronger relationships. If we keep isolating ourselves with technology, we risk losing the valuable social interactions that help us grow, both personally and as a community. I don't think it's constructive to keep moving in this direction. We need to prioritize real connections if we want to continue progressing.

I have tried to maintain a positive and resilient mindset despite life's challenges. I paint a picture of happiness, smooth sailing, and respecting others, but I know there will be times when things aren't easy. People will let you down in ways that hurt. Fortunately, those moments have been rare for me. It's not that I haven't been hurt or wronged in the past—I have. But I choose not to let it bother me because what's the point? What do we really gain from holding onto that hurt? I don't think I've ever hated someone. Hate is a very strong word, and honestly, I don't like the word "hate" at all. Why should I hate someone? I don't need to love them, see them, or talk to them. They're like footprints that come and go. Once they're gone, that's it. Holding on to grudges or hate only eats away at you. The thing is, it happens slowly, so you might not even notice it at first, but it's there, festering inside. Over time, it turns into anger and changes you, little by little, often without you realising. Don't give space to hate, it's a seed that grows into something worse, slowly poisoning your soul. There's no point in holding onto it. If someone is hurtful, mean, or difficult, just move away, disconnect, and let it go.

I tried to raise Luke to understand this. It is a message I hope he will not forget. I also tried to teach him to always be grateful for what you have. I remind him about my time in Belize, where people often went without food. I tell him not to take his food for granted. I remember seeing kids playing barefoot in the dirt, with barely anything, but they were full of joy. It made me think of kids here who have so much—PlayStations and the other latest gadgets—and yet, these children in Belize were just as happy, if not happier. I grew up in Sudan, which by all accounts was a country of hardship. But I was fortunate to grow up in a comfortable, even well-off, situation. I had a chauffeur to take me to school and back, and we had house help at home. But I also saw the other side of Sudan, such as severe poverty and the devastation of civil war.

I want Luke to know that there's no point in feeling jealous about what others have or what they've achieved. There's always someone out there who might be jealous of what you have and they don't. Instead of focusing on what you lack, be thankful for what you've got. If you really stop and look, you'll realize you're doing better than you think, and you already have everything you need. Don't waste time on envy or resentment because someone else has more. Instead, let it drive you. Use their success as motivation. If they made it, it's because they pushed themselves, so challenge yourself to do the same.

At the moment, Luke is obsessed with basketball and looks up to Steph Curry. When Curry misses shots, he'll say, "Steph Curry makes every shot!"

I tell him, "When Curry was your age, he probably missed a lot too. But he challenged himself every day, and that's why he's where he is. So, challenge yourself, don't just sit in jealousy." I think he understands. I want him to remember this and to help Sophia learn this too.

CHAPTER 18
MESSAGE TO MY COLLEAGUES

I do have a message for my colleagues in the NHS. This career that we have chosen goes beyond a regular job. I beg that people actually go into this role it because they understand what it means not just because it's a job and the minimum requirements are met. This might be a naïve opinion piece, but I believe that this career is a calling. If you ask a person one of the most important things to them, it's their health. We see people at their most vulnerable, their most worried, their most scared and fearful moments, and we have the honour of walking with them through this. You're not there to fill in paperwork. You are not there to fix the car so they can go to work. I am not belittling any of other jobs, but what I'm saying is that you're dealing with people, and people — no matter what walk of life, no matter what background — all have the same concern: health. We all want to be healthy. Then treating them with the dignity that they deserve, and the care that they deserve should always be our number one priority.

I think over time, unfortunately, within the NHS, we're losing that vision that at the end of the day, the patient is our primary concern. We're more worried about a host of other issues, be it defensive medicine, paperwork, bed space, etc. Lots of factors are clouding our vision. Yes, these factors need addressing, but they shouldn't take centre stage. We need to refocus. There's a lot of talk about the NHS breaking down due to budget cuts, lack of space, and issues in social care, but we can't let these challenges distract us. Don't let that take your vision, and don't let it take your purpose away. The external influence should not overpower the internal influence — the reason we decided to do the job.

I'd like to give an example. Once I was walking to work at the hospital, and outside the main entrance, I could see there was someone on the floor rolled in a ball, clearly in pain. This was just before 9 a.m., while everyone was walking into work. I could see people I recognized, and some were consultants, registered nurses, different professionals. I was sickened to my stomach by how many of them walked past this lady who was on the floor. They all just walked in through the door without batting an eyelid to look at her and ask, "Are you okay?" You don't need to be a specialist to recognise someone in distress; all you need is to be a human who cares. You don't have to be in healthcare to show that kind of compassion. But the fact that these individuals, who work in healthcare, were walking through the doors to care for patients while ignoring someone clearly suffering. It was deeply troubling. Honestly, I wish everyone who walked past had just turned around and gone home. Because if their response to seeing someone in pain was to walk on by, I wouldn't want any of them looking after me. It made me furious to my core. I was angry that we, as doctors and nurses, had reached a point where we could see someone in pain and simply walk by, all because we were more focused on getting the job done and going home.

A medical or nursing career, is not an easy path, it is not a 'normal' job. It takes over your life. It affects your family life. It is a big price to pay, but it's also the most rewarding thing. Especially now as I pass through this illness, I see the impact of the phenomenal work that is being done. There are some incredible doctors, incredible nurses, and other health staff out there. But I think there's others who have lost their way. If I could ask for anything, it is for those people who have lost their love for medicine, for nursing, to try again to find it.

We must always remember that the patient should be our top priority. Everything we do should revolve around the patient. There are simple things that often get overlooked, such as leaving patients connected to IVs for hours. To us, it may seem like no big deal, since we'll just disconnect it later. But for the patient, they're attached to this line, and when they need to go to the bathroom, they have to drag it along with them. Unless you've been in their position, you can't fully understand how frustrating it is to walk around with something that's no longer necessary, knowing it's just in the way. This may seem like a minor thing, but it's important to keep patients informed and involved. It's their body, and they have every right to understand what's happening and to be part of the decision-making process.

One of my pet peeves is when I am on call, and a nurse calls about a patient and asks, "Do you know Mr. So-and-so?"

And I'd have to respond, "No. I don't," because I'm on call and looking after the
whole hospital. "Can you tell me about him?"

Then, after a pause, they would start reading off two lines from the handover paper. That has always frustrated me. You're asking me if I know this patient, yet you've had a handover for every individual patient on your ward, and you should know them better than I do. But when I ask for details, you have to go back to the paper to read a couple of lines, most often noting things like "DNR" or "risk of falls," which don't really help me understand who the patient is or how to best advise you. Get to know your patients. That's the only way we can truly look after them and treat them holistically.

This message is especially true for doctors: Don't focus on the disease; focus on the patient. To be a little cheesy and quote a line from *Patch Adams*: "You treat a disease, you win, you lose. You treat a patient, you win no matter the outcome." I know it's a lame movie line, but it's something that I took as a way to practice medicine because I believe is true. That's what it comes down to—being a doctor means taking a proper history, engaging with the patient, and building a rapport, rather than just rushing through the process, desperate to move on to the next task or patient.

I understand the role of imaging and technology in modern medicine, and we have so much more to help us make decisions now. However, one thing we were taught in medical school is that by the time you finish taking a thorough history, you're 70% certain of the diagnosis. Only 20% comes from the examination, and the remaining 10% is from investigations. However, what I am seeing now on the medical clerking is two lines of history and just a plan for a CT, and this test and that test. When I read those histories, I get the immediate feeling that the doctor didn't really connect or build a rapport with the patient. That's not a way of practicing medicine. That's artificial intelligence. You are making yourself replaceable by removing the biggest and most valuable component of care that you provide. The patient's story will always tell you more. Go back to the basics. Ignore what CT, MRI, or blood tests you're going to order. Just take some time to know that patient. If you actually give the patient that time to talk and to listen, then often, the information you get is more than enough. I've always stressed that point throughout my teaching to my juniors. By the end of your history and examination, I expect three differential diagnoses, and I would grill them on the reasoning for these because a CT scan and its worth is linked to the entire clinical picture. Otherwise, you end up acting on the million incidental findings and actually miss why the patient was there in the first place.

Everything must work together and not be independent of each other. For that reason, your history with that patient must be your main priority, not just something you have to do because it's in the proforma or because you have to write two lines. Because the patient wants to tell you what's going on. If they already, from the beginning, feel that you didn't really bother or give them the time to tell you, whatever happens after that you've already lost them, and it just becomes more difficult to build rapport after that, since the patient lost faith in what you're doing. They might think, "I waited five hours in A&E to see a doctor who spent two minutes talking to me and then left the room." They waited only to have you rush in, barely looking up, offering no more than a couple of minutes before leaving them behind. What do they think of you? What do they think of the care they have received?

Another issue with rushing into medicine is that you might end up in a specialty that isn't the best fit for you. This could affect how well you perform as a doctor because your skill set and personality may not align with that specialty. When I was applying for specialty training, I took it for granted that you just pick one specialty. I thought, "If I like cardiology, I'll just apply for cardiology." I never even realized you could apply for multiple specialties. Then I spoke to some of my friends, and I was surprised to hear that some were applying for four different specialties: respiratory, cardiology, geriatrics, and others. I thought, "Wait a second. You can apply to more than one? What's your passion? You can't tell me you love all four equally." Picking a specialty because the competition ratios for jobs are more favourable shouldn't be the aim, the aim should be to harness your passion. Even though I started training in respiratory medicine, I eventually realized that acute medicine is my strength. I still enjoy respiratory medicine, but acute medicine is where I truly excel. Take the time to determine what you're passionate about is important, as well as what will make you the best doctor you can be, since that will shape how you feel about your job and how you do job.

I really hope that people get to experience the joy that comes with this journey, but it's not easy. If you're pursuing this simply because you have the A-levels or think it's an easy route, think again. Becoming a good or even great doctor is hard work. It's easy if you're okay with just getting by as an "average" doctor, but that's not the goal. The first year will be your steepest learning curve by far, but as time passes, things will get a little easier. Don't rush through it. A lot of people think they can take the quickest path to becoming a consultant, believing that's when everything gets easy. But let me tell you, being a consultant is not an easy life.

There's so much more responsibility involved. It's not just about making the final decisions and not having anyone else to pass them on to—it's about owning that responsibility. It's not an easy burden to bear. Plus, there's a lot of management work, not always clinical, that comes with being a consultant. It's part of your day-to-day job. If you think you'll just breeze through your training to reach that consultant position and then it's smooth sailing from there, think again. Sometimes, I honestly wish I were still a junior doctor instead of a consultant.

If you find yourself just going through the motions, whether in life or in medicine, take a moment to step back and reflect. Life and medical practice are meant to offer more than just routine. Each patient is unique, with different symptoms and needs. Rushing through their care only leads to mistakes. Medicine demands focus and personalized attention for every patient. If you fall into the habit of merely checking off tasks, you'll miss important details. Every patient deserves the time and care needed to avoid misdiagnoses and to ensure they receive the best treatment possible.

Yes, there are many patients, and they all need your care. They deserve your time. Even amidst the chaos of the emergency department, the fast-paced ward rounds, or the overwhelming flow of medical admissions, it's crucial that you give each patient the attention they deserve. Every single one of them. Some may seem like "time wasters"— those who might not need urgent medical intervention but come to the hospital out of fear, confusion, or desperation. They still deserve your care. They are vulnerable, scared, and need someone to guide them. You need to be that person for them.

There's nothing more rewarding than this career. After my religion and my family, medicine is the third love of my life. I've never regretted becoming a doctor. It has not been a smooth path, but I made it — and I'm so glad I did.

CHAPTER 19

THE FINAL CHAPTER

Throughout this book, you've seen what my life has been, the challenges I faced, the up the downs, and the things I have learnt. They all help shape the person I am. I also wanted to use this book to also share a bit of what I've learnt on this journey. After all, the tools I've used might be relevant to you. I am definitely not a guru that has the answers, nor am I here to tell you how to live your life. I'm just saying that this is my life. This is how I lived it. Something in it may be of value to you, and if it resonates, then the message is for you.

Life is short. When I had my first illness, that was my first real wake-up call. Life is short. If I hadn't experienced that illness, I probably wouldn't have bought the house, started the charity, or launched the business. I made decisions that might have seemed impulsive, but this was because I was made aware early on that life is short. Buying a house as a student was not the norm in those days. I opened a charity to give back in Belize, and although we had no savings, Jen and I found a way to live four months out of pocket. We came back and barely recovered, managed to open a business through determination. I remember discussing with friends what the next one project would be and the common consensus was probably a beach bar in Belize, which I was more than ready to take on.

I'll say it again: Life is short. Make the most of it and enjoy it, because before you know when it's over. Travel, travel, travel, travel, travel if you can. It's not cheap, but use alternative means, travel abroad, or travel to different parts of the country. Experience different cultures if you can. There's an incredible wealth of beauty in other cultures and places—not just in the scenery, but in the people, the food, the whole experience.

I love my food, and in so many cultures, it is a way to take time and connect. Take the Greeks, for example, and their meze. We often think of meze as a sampler platter—several small plates of food to try. But when you go to Greece and see it in action, it's something entirely different. People gather with family or friends, and that meze sits in the middle for hours. It's not just about eating quickly and moving on; it's an event. The food is there, yes, but it's part of the experience. They sit together, chat, laugh, reminisce, and graze through the plates over time. I love my food. With everything going on, losing my taste (even though it's a minor side effect compared to others) affected me greatly because I can't enjoy eating, which is something I enjoy so much. It's always been a great enjoyment for me trying different foods, different ways of doing things, cooking things, and experimenting with different ingredients. When we opened the restaurant, being able to tweak around with different ingredients and stuff was great fun — seeing the end product and savouring it.

Take time to grow as a person. I've always been a strong advocate for challenging yourself. I've pushed myself to learn how to open and run a charity, to practice medicine in a different country, and to survive for four months without getting paid. I challenged myself to learn how to start a business. Then I went on to become a gelato chef. I challenged myself again when I opened the restaurant portion, eventually running the kitchen and serving food that met restaurant standards. It's all about constantly pushing yourself, testing what you're really made of, and acquiring new skills. Because if you fall into a routine and become idle, it can eat away at you. I know once you have kids and responsibilities, it's easy to get stuck in that cycle, but it's important to keep growing and learning. I used to sit once a week, usually at night, and reflect in bed: What did I learn this week? What did I do that was different from last week? Did this week have something special? I'd always try to find something, and if I didn't, I'd get frustrated because it meant I hadn't challenged myself. That's when I'd decide to set a challenge for the next week. It could be something simple, such as learning to cook a new meal I liked, but it was still a challenge. I always made sure to challenge myself, and you should do the same: Always challenge yourself.

As a young person, and I know some parents might disagree, I truly believe you should encourage your kids to go away for university. That's where they really grow. I've seen both sides—those who stayed at home and those who left—and the difference is clear. Leaving home at 18 helps them gain independence and develop life skills they wouldn't otherwise. It's a crucial step in maturing and discovering who they are. University is a prime time for learning to cook, manage money, and take care of yourself. These are responsibilities you might not have had before, and moving away forces you to handle them. Staying at home can keep you in a routine, and you might miss out on those important life skills. Moving away helps you grow in ways staying home doesn't.

One thing that worries me about the world and our future is the change in the way we treat each other. It seems like we're always looking for reasons to treat others badly. We focus on their flaws—whether it's the color of their skin, their religion, their job, their background, or their age—and we use that as an excuse to mistreat, ignore, neglect, or avoid them. I've never understood why. The greatest commodity we have is each other. Our strength lies in numbers, in caring for one another, not in avoiding or attacking each other. It's baffling to me that we can be quick to react negatively, just because someone looked at us a certain way on the underground or something like that. Instead of jumping to a negative reaction, why not step back and ask ourselves, why is that our first instinct? It shouldn't be.

My message is simple. Love, trust, kindness are all great qualities. But for me, the number one is respect. Give everyone respect from the start. Sure, they might lose it later, but start with respect. Respect that everyone has their own struggles, their own lives, their own journey. You never know what they've been through to get to where they are. A simple gesture, such as walking down the street, nodding, or saying "good morning," can be a sign of respect. Like an army salute, these are immediate, easy ways to show respect.

Being generous can be tough if you don't have much to give, but respect is easy because you don't have to work at it. The first impression should always be respect.

You don't have to fall in love with the person but treat them with respect from the start. If they lose your respect later, that's different, but initial respect is key. When you show respect, people often return it. If you greet someone with a "good morning," they'll likely respond in kind, not with negativity. Whether we're talking about politics, religion or current issues like refugees, we need to treat everyone with respect. If you meet them at the point of anger, it doesn't mean that they're an angry person, you don't know what has happened to make them angry. So start with respect first, since you have no idea about their journey.

For Luke and Sophia I'd like them to remember that they will meet many people in life, and the impact on your life can be thought of as footprints. Some will come go and not leave any evidence, no footprints. Some will leave shallow footprints, these will be acquaintances, maybe some colleagues that you just have minor interactions with. These prints also disappear. Others you meet will leave slightly deeper footprints that will last a bit longer, but eventually over time, those fade away as well.

On the other side of the spectrum, however, there are people that will come into your life and leave a footprint that's almost set in cement. These are your friends; these are your family. You might be distant from them. They might move countries. Just because of life, you might not see them again. But there wouldn't be a day that passes by that you would have forgotten about them because they've left such an impression in your life that is set in stone that it becomes timeless in your memory. I look back and see that I am fortunate to have so many of these permanent footprints in my life. These are the people who have dropped everything when I needed them. I wish for you to have many of these people in your life as well.

It is easy to be generous with those that have helped and supported you, but I hope you will also find joy giving to those who may not thank you or reward you. Of course, I do everything within reason, but the act of giving—whether it's time, love, or something material—is incredibly rewarding. It's about putting others before yourself. It takes me back to my Christian values, to loving your neighbor as yourself and making others a priority. For most of my life, I've put people first, and I have no regrets. But the people I've put first have always deserved it.

Sometimes, I wonder if I should have been more selfish. If I should've just done what I wanted to do. But when I think about it, what I wanted was to put others first, and that, for me, was the win. Maybe it's not the same for everyone, but it's been true for me. I've always enjoyed being the host, organizing events, and making sure everyone feels welcome. People often ask, "Aren't you tired? Don't you just want to relax and do nothing?" But the truth is, being the host is something I genuinely enjoy. I love making sure people are having a good time, that they have food, drinks, and everything they need when they're at my house. Whether it's organizing trips, social events, or anything else, yes, it can be time-consuming, stressful, or nerve-wracking at times. But at the end of the day, it's what makes me happy. My ultimate goal is to make people happy every day, and putting them first is how I do it. Going out of my way to ensure they have what they need is what brings me the most joy.

Being a doctor has also given me the opportunity to make a real difference in people's lives. It's not just about the medical care; it's about going out of my way to listen to their stories and show that I care. That personal connection, the act of truly hearing them, always makes a difference and brings them happiness. This belief has shaped the way I live and resulted in a fulfilling life. The more I saw the impact I had on my patients, the happier I became. Their joy became my reward, my gift back for the effort I put in. It's always been my philosophy from day one—to give as much as I can and to make others happy.

People might call it brave, stupid, childish, or difficult, but to me, it was never hard. Even now, I serve with joy because it's simply who I am. To me, it was never difficult. To this day, I help otheres with joy because that's the only way to be I know how to be. That to me is my interpretation of Christianity and in how to be a Christian. God says that in His presence, there is fullness of joy. I have that joy ,and there's nothing I love more than sharing that with and making those around me happy. That's my version of Bible bashing, my "happy bashing."

For me, it all comes down to bringing who I am—my personality, my beliefs, how I was raised—and using that to bring a little happiness to other people. Put others first, and treat them with respect.

Now, as I find myself in need of support, I'm overwhelmed by the outpouring of love and care I've received. People have dropped everything — jobs, families, their own lives — to stand by my side. The messages I receive from work colleagues, friends, even from those across the globe, show me how far-reaching the happiness I tried to spread has gone. It tells me that my life has had meaning. My "happy bashing" has made a difference. So, when I think about what lies ahead, I'm not scared. I used to be upset about the thought of missing out on time with my kids, but now I feel at peace. I've accomplished what I set out to do, and that brings me comfort and strength during this time.

PART II
THEIR LIFE IN HER WORDS

CHAPTER 1

George and I first met properly in our fourth year of medical school, when I answered an advertisement for a house share. I had to move out of my current accommodation at the end of the year as none of my housemates were staying on. I saw his advertisement on the notice board outside the Michael Heron Lecture Theatre, where we had our lectures, and gave the number a call.

We arranged to meet up. The meeting went well, and I decided to move in. Funnily enough, it took a year or two to realise we had actually met before that. Back in second year, during freshers' week, George was manning the St. John Ambulance stall. I had tried to join, but he wouldn't let me. He said, "We're always full," or something cocky like that. I never let him live it down. "You're the one who stopped me joining St. John!" became one of our running jokes. With St George's being small university, our paths had crossed a few times, but we never spoke properly or connected until we shared a house.

I moved into George's house on Pevensey Road at the start of the fifth year for what turned out to be an eventful year. Functionally, it was slightly chaotic; for starters, George had no idea how to use the washing machine, despite living there for years, and sent me to ask another housemate! Socially, it was amazing. The house was a hub for meeting. We had a lot of karaoke nights among other events that made for some unforgettable memories.

A lot of alcohol was consumed. I remember one night we had finished all the many bottles George had on the kitchen windowsill and were disappointed until we found an old bottle of Jose Cuervo in a corner. We had no idea how long it had been there for, but with our judgement already impaired, we went for it. It had clearly concentrated over time because what followed was one of the most entertaining nights of the year as we all laughed, sang, danced and chatted until morning.

CHAPTER 2

Living together changed something in both of us. Over those first few months in the house, we got to know each other deeply. Still, it wasn't until the week before we left for our respective electives — me to Hong Kong, George to Toronto and then Belize — that he finally asked me out. Picture an 11–12 hour time difference: two separate worlds held together by phone calls and texts. I'd call him at 7 a.m. my time, walking to work at my hospital in Hong Kong; he'd be nursing his umpteenth cocktail in a bar halfway around the world. The timing was far from perfect, but that's how we started.

When we were finally back in the same country, two or three months later, we finally had our first "official" date. The time apart had only made our connection stronger.

One of our earliest challenges together as a couple was deciding where to live once we graduated. The job allocation system for junior doctors was complex and felt almost random at times. George had been allocated a job in Carmarthen in Wales for his F1, meanwhile I was working at St Peter's in Chertsey. Our relationship continued as long distance, me travelling on weekends to Carmarthen, or us meeting halfway in Bristol. When the time came to apply for specialty training, I chose surgery and applied for core surgical training in London, Bristol, and Wales. Unexpectedly, Wales was the only programme that offered me a place, so we embraced Wales, and Carmarthen became home. We rented a bigger, cheaper place, three times the size of my previous flat shares and began to build our lives together.

George proposed to me one night during a wonderful four-day cruise we had taken to the Bahamas. That evening we had docked, and it was the formal night for the dinner, so we were both dressed up: I in a nice dress and George in his suit. I remember he was acting odd, but I didn't think too much of it. I just assumed he had too many cocktails! He became particularly odd after dinner. We were outside, and it was chilly, but for once, he didn't immediately offer me his jacket. He shuffled around a fair bit before finally offering it to me. Little did I know, he didn't share was because the engagement ring was in the jacket pocket! When he proposed, it was perfect — the location, the moment, everything. I said yes instantly. I'd have said yes anywhere, though. I loved him so much, but all the thought and planning that he did elevated it several levels. He was amazing like that.

One of my favourite stories from our honeymoon happened on the way back from Tahiti and Bora Bora. We'd decided to stop off in Los Angeles for a few days because, of course, we were feeling fancy. After the prices of Bora Bora, LA felt like a bargain. I remember laughing when we realised a can of Coke in Bora Bora had cost us £5 and a packet of crisps was somehow even more expensive at £6! So when we landed in LA, expecting everything to be extortionate, we kept saying, "Oh my God, this is so cheap!" — a rare thing to say in Beverly Hills.

We were staying at the Hilton, and one afternoon we wanted to visit the local Westfield mall, which was only five minutes away. We asked the concierge how to walk there, the poor man looked at us as if we'd asked for his firstborn child. "You want to *walk*?" he said, horrified. "We'll call you a taxi."

We insisted. "Honestly, it's fine. Just point us in the right direction."

Still baffled, he gave us directions. We walked, of course, and had a good laugh about how deeply confused he'd been and how he could not understand why we would choose to walk there.

Another of our highlights of our time in LA was going to Universal Studios. We made our way through the haunted house attraction, the kind filled with actors jumping out at you in the dark, scaring you senseless. Now, I'm someone who screams through roller coasters from beginning to end, and George used to laugh his head off at me every time. This haunted house was no different. I was screaming before anything even happened, pre-emptively terrified. I clung to George's arm so tightly I probably cut off his circulation. By the time we came out the other side, he'd half-lost hearing in one ear, and the collar of his T-shirt was stretched halfway down his chest because I'd been yanking on it the whole time. He never let me live that down.

CHAPTER 3

One of our biggest projects together as partners was our big mission trip to Belize under the banner of our charity, Royal Blue Egg. Before the main mission, we went twice for shorter visits. The first trip was simply to get a feel for what was needed, to introduce ourselves, explore the area, and connect with the local hospital services. The second visit was more about making sure everything was in place before we committed to the longer stay, checking that the hospital setup would work and that it all felt right. Each of those trips lasted about a week, and both were lovely in their own way. They helped us see that this was something we could really do together.

With George, once an idea took hold, that was it — he was all in. That was just how he was, whether it was a restaurant idea, a gelato shop, or Belize itself. When something captured his imagination, it became a vision he couldn't let go of. His enthusiasm was infectious, and it felt like the right time. We didn't have children yet, and I had just finished CT2 in core surgical training and was ready for a pause. I also knew how much Belize meant to George; it had stayed with him ever since his elective. He talked about it constantly. I didn't want him to regret not going. So I thought, "You know what? It's only a few months. Let's give it a try. If it doesn't work out, we can always come back."

So we committed ourselves fully to the venture and worked hard to make it happen. It wasn't easy, of course. Financially, it was a real challenge; we were funding it ourselves. I did a lot of locum shifts beforehand to save up, making sure we had enough for the three months we would be there. There was a lot of planning involved, fundraising, organising equipment, and shipping everything over. Looking back at all the difficulties — getting the charity off the ground, sorting out logistics, seeing the mission through — I still marvel at how we did it all. It was one of the most intense and fulfilling times of our lives. It tested us in the best ways and, without a doubt, brought us closer than ever.

We always lived by the motto "Work hard, play hard." In Belize, that meant making the most of our weekends. One of our favourite places to visit was a little peninsula called Placencia. It was quiet, quaint, and at that time not yet overrun by tourists. We absolutely loved it. There was this amazing gelato shop we found there, run by a lovely German-French couple. We ended up going there at least twice a day and got to know the owners well. That little shop ended up inspiring the gelato shop we would open later. We also took trips out to the coast to go scuba diving, and the reefs off Belize were stunning. Those weekends exploring the country, discovering places together, were some of my favourite memories from the whole experience.

CHAPTER 4

One of our sillier stories comes from a short trip George and I took to Lisbon, back when it was just the two of us. True to form, George had booked us into a posh hotel, the kind with all the bells and whistles, including a fancy espresso machine that hadn't yet made its way to the UK. For some reason, I felt the need to try the strongest pod available — the Ristretto, with an intensity level of 10. I'm not sure why I thought that was a good idea. I'm notoriously caffeine-sensitive, unlike George and his family, who basically drink gunpowder as coffee.

Within minutes of downing that tiny espresso shot, I was completely wired. George genuinely thought the coffee had been spiked. I became obsessed with this tiny gap in the curtains and — don't ask me how or why — ended up inventing a full-on song called "A Hole in the Curtain," which I performed, enthusiastically, for the next hour. George was in stitches.

I told the story to Luke recently, and he just stared at me like I'd lost the plot. But to this day, it's one of those moments we always laughed about: me, high on caffeine, singing nonsense about curtains in a luxury hotel.

We had some scary moments too. I remember when we went to Cancun, again before we had children. We decided to swim in the sea. The waves were wild and high, but we were young and carefree, and we went in anyway. While we were in the water, I saw a large wave coming. I grabbed George's hand and said, "Don't let go, no matter what." Of course, the moment the wave hit, he let go, and I was tossed about 20 or 30 feet down the beach, rolling in sand and swearing at him the whole time. Terrifying at the time, but ever since, it's been a running joke: me complaining, "Remember I told you not to let go! You let go and I went flying," and him responding, "You should be more worried — you almost lost me that day!"

Back at home in Carmarthen, we had an active social life that kept us busy between trips to London to see family. When we opened the restaurant, life became hectic, and we were both exhausted, but George still made times for friends, with entertainment continuing whether at home or in the restaurant bar. We were also part of a tight knit hospital community; everyone knew and liked George, his knowledge, willingness to teach and approachability meant he was popular and held in high esteem by everyone.

The only time we worked together on a shift resulted in one of the funniest work memories. We were both working a shift in Accident and Emergency: I the Registrar and he the locum SHO. Suddenly, the dreaded bat phone went off with news of a train derailment. Instantly, we pictured a massive high-speed disaster, mass casualties, the works. The whole department began to clear out, preparing for the worst. We all ate quickly and gathered in the central area of the department, anticipating a large casualty influx. An additional call soon came through. There was a pregnant woman and a child involved. The tension rose; this was serious. Minutes passed. No patients arrived. We exchanged confused glances. What was going on? Finally, the truth came out: it wasn't a full-blown train derailment at all. It was a small amusement park toy train — the kind that kids ride on at Pembrey Park — that had jumped the tracks. We all burst out laughing. Here we were, suited up for a disaster, and it was just a miniature train ride gone off course. It wasn't quite the big ER moment we had envisaged.

CHAPTER 5

George's parents were the foundation of the family. His mum is one of the sweetest people I know — always fussing over whether you've eaten, instantly making you feel welcome the moment you walk through the door. Her way of caring is so genuine and comforting. His dad is more reserved, though definitely someone you respect the moment you meet him. He's mellowed a lot over the years; when I first met him, he had this presence, a kind of quiet authority. The best way I can describe it is like an orthopaedic consultant you wouldn't want to cross — calm, composed, but with an edge of command. There was just that energy about him. But especially now, when I see him with our kids, Luke and Sophia, it's a completely different side. There's a gentleness in the way he interacts and plays with them. It has been beautiful to see that relationship evolve over time.

One of my favourite funny memories involving George's

parents happened not long after we'd moved into our house in Wales. That first weekend, we drove down to London to visit family, and after a long day, we finally collapsed into bed at their place, completely exhausted.

Around 3 a.m., George suddenly shook me awake.
"Jen," he whispered, dead serious.
"What?" I mumbled, still half-asleep.
"There's someone in the house."
In our groggy haze, we both completely forgot we were in London, not Wales, and panicked.
I sat up, heart racing. "Call the police!" I whispered. "Call 999!"

George grabbed his phone, ready to do exactly that, and paused suddenly. Then it hit him: we were at his parents' house. This was completely normal. In fact, in their house, nobody went to bed before 3 a.m. He put the phone down, turned to me and said, "Never mind . . . it's just my parents."

We lay there in silence for a moment with me completely unimpressed by being shaken to my core. But now? We both laugh every time we tell the story. When we got back to Wales, though, just to be safe, despite no break-ins, I went out and bought an aluminium baseball bat. It still lives under the bed to this day, just in case.

George and his brothers had a bond that was built on years of childhood antics and shared memories. The kind of sibling relationship full of inside jokes, harmless teasing, and stories that only make sense to them. They were always getting into some sort of mischief when they were younger, and even though they've grown into very different people with different lives, that connection is still there. There's a kind of unspoken understanding between them. Whatever life throws their way, they'll figure it out together. That's just who they are.

Sami and Nisreen are technically cousins, but they've always felt more like brother and sister to George. Nisreen was a big source of support to George especially in his early years in the UK. That bond has endured. Sami, in particular, has been a constant presence in George's life. They were always together growing up, and even into adulthood, remained incredibly close. The two of them together was a recipe for chaos, particularly if there was any kind of celebration involved. There is one story when George and Sami once had a night out in Cardiff, just the two of them, not a combination that signals a quiet evening. They both ended up at a rum bar. They had a great time, but by the end of the night, someone had been sick, on a mattress no less, and George was left to deal with the hotel bill. No one knows exactly what happened, and that's probably for the best, but it was classic George and Sami: total carnage, but in the best possible way.

The football banter between the two of them was endless. George, a loyal Chelsea supporter, and Sami, a die-hard Manchester United fan, never missed a chance to wind each other up, especially when one team was slipping in the Premier League. The teasing was often hilarious. It was a friendly rivalry, and it was always fun to watch them go back and forth, half-serious, half-laughing. This rivalry extended to their PlayStation games, including FIFA and Call of Duty, which often went on into the early hours. It started long before the children came along, but somehow, even after, they still found time to play.

I remember one trip to Tenerife with Sami and his family; his wife, Sunita and their two children. Sophia was just a baby at the time, maybe two or three months old. Luke was older, full of curiosity and already developing very strong opinions about things. It was an all-inclusive resort, and while that sounded great in theory, Luke quickly grew tired of the buffet lunches. "I can't eat chicken nuggets and chips every day," he said, completely unimpressed. He's always been a bit of a food connoisseur—even as a little boy. They were fun times that were also essential to us staying connected and part of each other's lives. We try to stay connected, even with some of us living in different corners of the world now. There's comfort in that kind of closeness, in knowing that our children are growing up with that same sense of family.

George had a real love for cocktails, both drinking them and making them. One of the drinks he proudly introduced to Sami to was the infamous Beverly Hills Iced Tea, which is a Long Island Iced Tea, five spirits and a splash of mixer, but instead of cola, it's topped off with champagne — in other words, pure alcohol in a glass. One drink, and you were done for the night. Naturally, for George and Sami, it became a bit of a challenge to see who could drink one and still function without either vomiting or doing something ridiculous. Neither had a great track record.

One of their favourite haunts in London was Trader Vic's at the Hilton on Park Lane—sadly, now closed. After a night out in the city, we'd often end up there for "posh cocktails." Their drink of choice? The Queen's Park Swizzle. Tall, potent, and made with overproof rum and Angostura Bitters, not exactly sweet or forgiving. It was so strong that George and Sami used to nibble on the mint garnish just to get through the taste. It was hilarious watching them both sip away and slowly descend into tipsy chaos — very cheap dates, the both of them.

George's cocktail enthusiasm didn't stop at bars; he brought it home too. After a big get-together in Hampton, once the food was cleared away and people started to relax, George's home bar would open. He loved mixing up concoctions, often using Sunita and Sami as his unofficial taste-testers. Sunita, in particular, was a tough critic. George only managed to impress her a handful of times, but it didn't stop him from trying. There were always lots of laughs, a few questionable flavour combinations, and more than one hangover.

There was also his flavoured rum phase. He made it his mission to collect every single variation he could find; pineapple, mango, strawberry. Pirate Bay was a particular favourite. When we went to Miami, he was delighted to find new flavours and brought back bottles like they were rare treasures. He'd line them up, experiment with mixing, and serve them at parties, often to unsuspecting guests. It always started as a fun night and usually ended in a bit of a mess. Looking back, those nights were George in a nutshell, bringing people together, creating bonds and filling the room with friendship and laughter.

CHAPTER 6

When our son Luke was born, we were quite anxious. Early in my pregnancy, around five or six weeks, I experienced a small bleed, which was understandably worrying. To complicate matters, I was later diagnosed with placenta previa. Fortunately, I did not have any further bleeding episodes, but we remained cautious throughout the pregnancy. Being first-time parents, we were also filled with the excitement and anticipation of not knowing whether Luke would be a boy or a girl — a fact that, while thrilling for us, greatly frustrated George's parents, who were eager to find out. I was determined that we would keep the gender a surprise, and that added to the sense of mystery and excitement surrounding Luke's arrival.

Choosing a name proved to be surprisingly challenging. For a girl, we had already settled on the name Octavia, inspired by a strong character in a television series George was watching called *The 100*. While it might sound somewhat unconventional, the name felt fitting and meaningful. As we didn't have a name for a boy, I turned to the Synaxarium, the Coptic calendar of saints and significant religious figures, in search of inspiration. George was away on a night shift at the time, and I remember feeling the urgency to decide. We wanted a name that was meaningful but not overly common, so we decided against names like John or Mark. Then, I came across Luke, the patron saint of doctors. The name resonated with us, especially given our medical backgrounds. After some reflection, we agreed it was the perfect choice.

Luke was born by Caesarean section, and from the very start, George absolutely adored him. At first, Luke didn't want much to do with George, he wanted his mommy, of course, the one with the milk. But as Luke grew, he realized George was far more fun, and the bond between them grew rapidly. Soon after Luke was born, we opened the gelato shop downstairs, which was a huge amount of hard work. Luke loved visiting the shop and, naturally, loved the gelato. He was so proud of George's "ice cream shop" that he would tell all his friends at nursery, "Daddy has an ice cream shop," which was incredibly sweet.

As for George's relationship with Sophia, it's important to mention the heartbreak we faced between Luke and Sophia. I had two miscarriages: one just after ten weeks and another at sixteen weeks. Both devastated us. We never wanted to blame each other; it was just an incredibly difficult time filled with uncertainty. After the first miscarriage, we hoped the initial twelve-week scan would mark a safer point, but the second miscarriage proved otherwise. During a sixteen-week checkup, the midwife couldn't find a heartbeat. That news was crushing. After a long break and much discussion, we decided to try for one more baby, knowing if it didn't work out, we would accept it.

The pregnancy with Sophia wasn't easy either. The anxiety from the previous losses stayed with me throughout the pregnancy, but physically it went well — until the very end. Hoping for a natural birth after one C-section, I was ready to push. But Sophia, being a strong-willed second child and a girl, lived up to the stereotype: stubborn and determined. She was in a transverse lie and refused to move, so another C-section was necessary.

George adored Sophia as well, but just like with Luke, she was initially very attached to me. It wasn't until she grew a little older that she started showing her affection for George, wanting to spend time with him and cuddle him. It was truly heartwarming to see her personality bloom and to watch the bond between them grow. George loved them both fiercely.

CHAPTER 7

No one prepares you for the part where everything changes. When it came to George's final illness, it was incredibly difficult. I knew I had to stay strong, not just for him, but also for the children. Emotionally, it really was a roller coaster from start to finish. We were in and out of hospital constantly, barely catching our breath. The longest stretch he spent at home without being admitted was only six or seven days. For someone like George, who had already spent a significant part of his twenties battling serious illness, being in hospital again was especially tough. He hated it. We did everything we could to keep him out of hospital for as long as possible.

Our friends here in Carmarthen were brilliant and truly stepped up, and I'll always be grateful for that. My friends May and TJ made sure they were always available whenever I needed them. Our work teams were also truly supportive during those difficult times.

Despite how hard those months were, I don't think George had any regrets. He really did live life to the fullest. Belize, the restaurant, the gelato shop — we crammed so many of his dreams into such a short space of time. That was always our way: to throw ourselves into things and make them happen while we could. He'd always dreamed of opening a little bar in Belize, and even though we didn't get to do that exactly, we came close. We had the restaurant, the gelato shop, and even a bar here in Carmarthen. I'm so glad we made those things a reality. They mattered to him deeply.

As for the illness itself, it came as a shock to all of us. He was well and fit — until what seemed like a persistent chest infection that started to wear him down. It just wouldn't clear. From there, things escalated far more quickly than any of us expected. It felt like we were constantly clutching at straws, hoping for something to turn around. But near the end, I think we both began to understand, quietly, that this wasn't going in the direction we'd hoped for. Even then, he was still himself — still cracking jokes and staying optimistic, still more worried about how I was coping than himself.

The end came far, far too soon. It has left us all broken. The pain of his absence will always stay with me, but so will the joy of having known him and having achieved all that we did. George loved without limits, and though we've had to let him go, his love remains at the heart of our family and in the lives of the people he touched.

AFTERWORD

George passed away peacefully on the Sunday, 28 July 2024, surrounded by family.

There was so much more George wanted to include in his autobiography. Some significant stories and names are not included here, as the purpose of the book shifted in his final days — becoming less about precisely documenting and more about capturing the essence of who he was.

As his friends and family, we now share a responsibility to reinforce all that is here and to ensure that Luke and Sophia come to know their father more deeply through these stories, memories, and love for him.

We initially disagreed with George about the title of the book. We joked that he should consider naming it "The Man Who Moved to Wales to Open an Ice-Cream Shop" because that was George personified: seeing potential everywhere and optimistic in everything. Nothing was impossible or too crazy for him, not even a gelato shop in the wettest corner of Wales.

Although his health was medically complex, as the title alludes, George's spirit was pure and uncomplicated. He lived with a simple grace, loving others freely and generously.

What he leaves behind is his story — a legacy and a message of love. It's for Luke and Sophia above all, but it is also for anyone who was lucky enough to have known him.

PART III

REFLECTIONS — HIS LIFE IN OUR WORDS

REFLECTIONS

George lives on in the memories, stories, and love of those who knew him. The tributes that follow are written by friends, some who knew him from childhood, some through work, and others through chance encounters that turned into lasting friendships.

Luke and Sophia, these words are for you. They are here to help you see your father through the eyes of the many people who loved him. Just as this book preserves his voice, these reflections preserve his impact on those who knew him.

Writing these words in the shadow of loss is both a privilege and a heartbreak. George was my dear friend. We first met at church—two young people learning how to serve, grow, and walk by faith—and from the very beginning, his presence shone brightly. There was a quiet depth to him even then, wrapped in humour, creativity, and a kindness that ran deep.

Later, our paths crossed again in medical school, where we were fuelled with curiosity and caffeine. I had the joy of witnessing George not only grow into his calling as a doctor, but do so with the same humility and compassion he brought to every part of his life. Whether in a lecture hall, a hospital corridor, or a church pew, George was the same: generous, thoughtful, and full of life.

In fairness, to say George was full of life feels like an understatement. He radiated joy. His laughter was infectious, his optimism unwavering, and his creativity boundless. He had a gift for making people feel seen and valued, always choosing to view others through a lens of grace. He did this with such total commitment that you couldn't help but believe in the best version of yourself through his actions and friendship.

George faced challenges with remarkable courage. His spirit always remained fierce and light-filled. His humour endured, as did his faith, and his love for those around him never wavered.

To his beautiful wife, Jen, and his two precious children: George held a deep love and pride for you. You were his greatest joy, his home, and his heart. He lives on in each of you—in your stories, your strength, and in the love you carry forward.

It's hard to say goodbye. But it's easy to give thanks—for the gift of George, for all the ways he made the world lighter and better, and for the reminder he gave us daily: to live fully, love deeply, and walk humbly.

Rest well, dear friend. You are deeply missed and forever remembered.

Claire Badawi

George always put others before him. Hie was kind and had a way of making me feel included. I am grateful our lives crossed and what his friendship has taught me. Remembering you, George.

Jeanette Goh

———··•··———

It was a serious exam. We were assembled in one of the upstairs teaching rooms, anxiously waiting to be filed in to meet our simulated patients, interpret their x-rays, palpate a plastic manakin maybe. George glanced over at me and gave a smile both reassuring and mischievous. Quietly, he said, "Wow, everyone looks so serious." Saying no more, he pulled over a computer-on-wheels (later to be known as COWs) and calmly logged in, opened Internet Explorer, waited patiently before finding YouTube. He glanced over again, more mischievous than reassuring this time.

"Do you think…?" He began. "Well, anyway…" he said, trailing off into a chuckle.

Suddenly, the eerie mask from one of the *Saw* films appears on the screen ,and before I fully clock what George had in mind, the theme music begins to fill the room — ominous, foreboding. And it doesn't come from the computer, it pours out of the lecture speakers. Respectfully, George adjusts the volume. A room of confused medical students try to locate the music as the spooky melody takes hold. Something to lighten the mood. George laughed. And he's right – the room, stiff with apprehension, quickly relaxed, and serious faces broke into smiles.

This captures so much of my experience with George. He knew how to connect to people, how to put people at ease. Love and humour came easily to him. He knew how to lighten those intense and anxious moments – and medical school was full of them. I'd often ask him, "Why aren't you more worried about exam results… placements… what comes next?"

He might joke in response: "Why? It's St George's. It's my university!"

Sometimes he'd be more philosophical. He'd talk about being in and out of hospital, and say, "You learn what's in your control and what's not." Have faith, he seemed to be saying. In those last few months of medical school, I don't think he (or I) fully appreciated just how much getting through finals (and re-sits!) was thanks to George's easy kind of faith.

Connecting to others and helping them find a way through was only a part of it. George also connected people to each other. It wasn't unusual to drop by and see George at university only to find some of his other friends (or family!) already there. Setting up and hosting the weekly Christian group (FOCUS) seemed so easy for him. I remember Bishop Angelos sat in George's living room having a chat with his housemates. There are so many ways this could go wrong, I thought. But not George. For George, this was what loving connection was all about and even the most unlikely gatherings never went wrong. That loving connection was palpable – sometimes literally! Sometimes he couldn't tell you something without holding your arm or putting his arm around your shoulder. He never hid his love and enjoyment of being close to people. I saw the same thing in Luke when I met him.

It's hard to describe the warmth that George created in his home at university. It's an understatement to say that his way of being was unguarded, unselfconscious. Friends who barely knew George could suddenly find themselves in his home with their feet up in front of an episode of *Smallville*. No matter where you'd just come from, or how long you were staying, George made you feel at home. "Come over any time," he'd say, and you might find him in the kitchen cooking eggs in his gallabiyah. He was totally at ease with himself. George was that friend who, without saying a word, always let you know that you could relax, you could always be yourself, you were always welcome.

George didn't let anything get in the way of this. Being overly concerned with appearances was just pretence and a barrier to closeness, as far as George was concerned. For one of our year group photos at university, George was unwell and was admitted to one of the wards. This didn't stop him. He came down with a cannula in his arm and joined his year, smiling in front of the university entrance. Years later, when he invited me to the grand opening of his new gelato shop in Wales, I wondered what he had planned. Might there be a ribbon-cutting? I got there and George handed me a hammer and asked me to finish the beading round the skirting boards. We were together. We were a part of something shared and important. That's what mattered. We knew it, and we felt it. He was grateful, generous in whatever ways he could be which, in this instance, included Ferrero Roche gelato. Words cannot describe that gelato.

All of this was there, too, that last time I saw George shortly before he passed. "Dude! What do you think of the new look?" he said while stroking his chin and head. He told me about his recent cruise with Jen, Luke and Sophia. He showed me pictures and videos, as always wanting his experience to be shared and wanting to bring others in. He told me about writing this book and wanting his life to go on being shared with his children. It was impossible not to be moved by his determination to be present for those he loved. In that easy and understated way, he helped me to think more about those around me, my father, my connections, and my losses. And in that funny, faithful way of his, continuing to give more, and to touch more deeply than he realised.

John Gossa

When I first arrived at St George's, I realized I had a cousin there named George—but I hardly knew him. Little did I know how much our relationship would grow. What started as a cousin I barely knew quickly turned into a friend—and, ultimately, a big brother who was always there.
Like real siblings, we tested each other's patience (he pushed me to the brink of insanity more than once). One memorable night, I cooked a full three-course meal before he casually mentioned he was "allergic to mushrooms" — a so-called allergy I later discovered was anything but true!

George had a special talent for bringing people together. He built a tight-knit group of friends that felt like family. He was caring, generous, and always willing to help—no matter how big or small the favour, with no expectation or hesitation. Sometimes, even before you asked, he was already there.

Though we lost touch over the years, the memories we shared are timeless—and always will be.

Julie Hanna

My memory of your Dad/George at Medical School was that he always had a big smile, a giggly laugh that you just had to join in. And he was always bringing people together . . . lots of people, lots of food, and lots of fun. That ranged from BBQs and movies at his place to going out to Nandos, which was often a favourite to celebrate friends' birthdays. I was often busy working a job or two whilst studying Medicine, and I remember your Dad/George inviting me along to Nandos for a friend's birthday. I couldn't afford to go out for the meal, so I said I would eat at home and come join after for a drink. He wouldn't take no for an answer, and I can't remember if he paid for my meal or got others to chip in too. I will always remember him for his kind generosity – not just financially, but time, friendship, listening ear. He was a good man and a man of faith who would encourage us to meet and talk about God. Your Dad/George really was a remarkable man and is truly missed. May the Lord bless you and keep you; the Lord make his face shine on you and be gracious to you; the Lord turn his face toward you and give you peace (Numbers 6: 24-26). God bless you.

Fatima Larkin

George loved to host: food, cocktail making, Bible study, movie nights. You name it, George would be organising it in a second. And not just anyhow, he would make sure that he would line up the best of the best for whatever he was doing, and he made everything an experience. I never understood how he had that much energy for all these things and for people in general. He explained it to me very simply one day: "I enjoy making people happy." And he definitely did that without fail. Not just by organising events but in the small things too. He could be counted on to check on you if you hadn't been in touch for a while, and he would be first to notice if someone was not themselves and go to the end of the world to put it right. He cared deeply about his family, and he treated his friends as if there were immediate family. I used to tell him that I wasn't worthy of his friendship, so big was his heart and generosity. His faith was central to his life, and he truly lived it out in all he did, sharing and encouraging all of us in our faith. I was blessed to have been part of your life, George. I will miss you more than you know.

Charlotte

I first met George when I started at St George's Hospital Medical School in 2002. The premise of the intro was "another Coptic guy at St. George's." Within days, he'd generously loaned me a stack of medical textbooks — immaculate condition, suspiciously pristine. That was the start of a long friendship with someone who quietly but profoundly shaped my life.

George may have been one of the earliest adopters of remote learning — interestingly, well before lectures were available online. But this just freed him up to fully embrace his key strength: socialising. He seemed to know everyone. And everyone knew him.

He was bubbly, bright, and full of beans. His distinctive laugh could be heard across the "George's bar." He had a radar for fun and a generous instinct to include others in it. If there was football, he'd be in his kit. If there was a dance floor, he'd be tearing it up.

When he moved to his house in Pevensey Road, it quickly became his base and HQ for many of our social activities. George loved to host. And we loved being hosted. Movie nights, karaoke ("Zombie" by The Cranberries, of course), cocktails, and games. Many unforgettable memories in that house.

I'll always remember George for his warmth, his generosity, and his gift for bringing people together. He loved people, laughter, and occasionally letting me test out experimental recipes on him — most notably the infamous Balti Sausages (which, I think he liked!?).

Rest well, my dear friend. You brought a lot of joy to those around you. Until we meet again.

Michael Michail

———··•··———

George and I go way back. We met on a church trip when we were around 12. This was the prehistoric era, before mobile phones, when you'd actually have to call someone's house and speak to their parents (terrifying, I know). We'd agree on a time and place to meet, and then just stand awkwardly on the street like weird little time travellers waiting for the other to show up. Simpler times.

A few years later, we levelled up to pagers. Yep, pagers. We'd send each other messages that were 50% jokes, 50% insults, and 100% worth it.

After high school, we somehow both landed in the same college. We even shared a few classes, including A-level maths, where we sat side by side for 2 years. George started off being my study saviour, patiently explaining the assignments and topics. By the end of the year, we had a new system: he did the homework, and I expertly copied it.

Post-class, we had a routine: hit up the "all you can eat" buffet at Pizza Hut in Queensway (and oh, we could eat), then roll ourselves to the cinema. When we weren't stuffing ourselves in public, we were at his place doing the same thing. Pizza Hut delivery, movies on loop, and me passed out on his parents' sofa like it was my second home. Honestly, those were some of the best days.

As we got older, we travelled on holiday together, and he remained the same person I always knew even as an adult — cheeky, smiley, generous and a huge Chelsea fan. I cannot explain the number of times we would go out and he'd be wearing his Chelsea football shirt. Although we saw each other less frequently as we each started our own families, he was a one-of-a-kind friend who would pick up the conversation as if we had just seen each other the day before and always with a smile.

George will always be a big part of my story — gone from sight, but absolutely impossible to forget. He left behind a lifetime's worth of laughs, memories, and inside jokes that still crack me up – "hozbital".

Michael Takla

I will never forget his generosity and his amazing passion for life. Our crazy journey through medical school and precious time in Belize

Kwok Tsang

You never think that you will have to write a tribute about a great dear friend so early on in life. If anyone knows George in the ways that many of us did then you will know only too well what an amazing person George was and the ways in which he has touched every single one of our lives.

I met George at St George's Medical school; he was a biomedical sciences student at the time. A friend, a son, a brother, a husband, a father, a man of Faith, a doctor and one of the best comedians. Through the years at medical school George actively took part in so many different things but the University shows with dance and comedy and Discos are what stand out the most in my mind. George shared his funny side and creativity with everyone. He truly Danced like nobody was watching, loved like he would never be hurt, and sang even if no one was listening....he loved his karaoke.

Everybody knew him and for many reasons, George was kind, welcoming, funny, intelligent, and a strong person. He was one of the most decent men that I had the honour of knowing, respectful, cultured and well brought up. If he wasn't studying, he was training students and friends that needed help to prepare for exams, other times he would be helping out in the hospital, and if anyone ever needed something or a helping hand George was there whole heartedly doing what he could, albeit dealing with his own health issues always with a smile on his face and a heart full of love and joy.

If you were friends with George you more than likely where invited to one of the many famous get togethers and or BBQs, here is where many of us where introduced to the Coptic Church and wider community. We were introduced to a whole community of family and friends and on many occasions attended the Coptic church for ceremonies and celebrations. I cannot count the amount of times we have all fasted together. George was very committed to his faith and the community and through this many of us gained many other friendships and much more.

As with George his parents and brothers where always welcoming, loving and warm so it was no surprise when George met and fell in love with Jen. I can remember their wedding day and the video they shared with friends and family of their journey and relationship. The room was filled with, joy, laughter and love. Over the years George and Jen went onto create a beautiful family and I know that when both the children were born it was one of the most proudest moments of George's and Jens life.

We can never know God's plan and I am sure that many of us have asked why? George gone to soon, but in the time that I have knew George I can say that he lived a full and wonderful life. Even in the face of difficulty his faith and the love that he gave to everyone and the legacy and memories he leaves behind shine bright like the light that he is.

I know that George has left a huge void in everyone's life especially for Jen, the children and his family, but I hope that the memories, the love ,the laughter and legacy and light that he has left behind forever brings a smile and warmth to your heart as it does mine.

Salima Walji

Karaoke nights with George were unforgettable, not because he could sing (he absolutely couldn't), but because he gave it everything he had. His go-to? 80s power ballads, belted out with 100% energy and zero shame. It was his signature move to try and charm the ladies, which rarely worked, but his exaggerated and deliberately comical efforts always had us in stitches. George was the kind of person who didn't mind being the joke if it meant everyone else was laughing. He had this gift for making people feel good, included, and entertained — whether he was pouring drinks, telling stories, or checking in on the quietest person in the room. He was generous in every way that mattered, with his time, his wallet, and his love. I'm lucky to have known him and even luckier to have called him a friend.

Anonymous

George was very active in society and social life at his namesake university St George's. He was Chair of St John Ambulance amongst others which meant that he was out all the time organising first-aid cover for events all over south England, running first aid and basic life support courses as well as fund raiser activities for the society. He did this with the same passion he did everything with, and it earnt him an army of friends. He was never too busy to help anyone, and he would absolutely go out of his way if a friend was in need. This led some to take advantage of him, but that never deterred him. His impact on me was immeasurable, and I am so grateful to have known him.

Anonymous

www.ingramcontent.com/pod-product-compliance
Lightning Source LLC
Chambersburg PA
CBHW071118160426
43196CB00013B/2614